TABLE OF CONTENTS

W0010924

INTRODUCTION

Guinness World Records™ Reading gives students the opportunity to shatter their own records—reading records, that is! Just as ordinary people can become Guinness World Record holders, students can become world record readers when they experience the excitement of *Guinness World Records™ Reading*. Designed for struggling or reluctant readers, students on grade level, and high achievers, *Guinness World Records™ Reading* helps improve reading comprehension skills and motivates students to do their best.

What does it mean to be the best? Guinness World Record holders know! Some of them are people, such as the man who crashes cars for a living. Some are insects, such as the bug that makes a sound so high that nobody can hear it. Some record-holders are even buildings and robots! In this book, the more than 50 stories chronicle the triumphs of people, animals, nature, science, and technology. Their feats and successes are thrilling, and their records will amaze and inspire readers of all ages.

4

IN THIS BOOK

Guinness World Records™ Reading is divided into five themed units, with each unit highlighting incredible achievements in a specific category. Some of the records are exciting, some are unsettling, and some of them are just plain unbelievable—but, they are all extraordinary!

In the first unit, discover **Amazing Animals**, big and small: Meet a giant dog named George, a lizard with a deadly, monstrous bite, and a high-jumping pig. You will even meet a couple of law-enforcing animals. Who knew a camel could be a deputy?

In the next unit, explore records in **Engineering, Science & the Body**: Walk through a door large enough for a rocket ship, see a teenage girl who towers above the rest, check out a woman who can pop her eyes right out of their sockets, and meet a man who has been growing his fingernails for almost 50 years. Absolutely record breaking!

Experience the intensity of our home planet in **Earth Extremes**: Meet a park ranger who has been struck by lightning seven times, get lost in a 2.5 mile (4 km) Hawaiian maze, and visit a planet where a day is longer than a year. If that's not extreme, then what is?

Game Time! is sure to get you moving: Hop in a speedy go-kart for a 24-hour ride, swim the length of the Amazon River, and ride a 33-foot-long (10-m-long) snowboard. You'll be at the bottom of the mountain before you know it!

Just when you think you have heard it all, the **Wild, Wacky & Weird** proves you haven't: One record-breaker made a car-sized rubber band ball, another holds rattlesnakes in his mouth, and yet another took his riding lawn mower for a 14,594-mile (23,487-km) spin across the country. Wacky? The wackiest!

HOW THIS BOOK WORKS

Guinness World Records™ Reading provides parents and educators with materials and experiences that make reading compelling and fun for students. More than 50 short passages offer subject matter that motivates and engages even the most reluctant students to read, write, and explore fascinating topics. Each high-interest, grade-level reading passage is based on an actual Guinness World Record. Students will become world record readers as they absorb astounding content, expand their vocabulary, and add to their knowledge of unusual facts and inspiring people.

Refer to each themed unit to select subjects of specific interest to your students, or choose subjects based on units within your curriculum. Use the matrix to identify the skills that each lesson targets. Achievement of each skill varies, depending on the depth of knowledge students demonstrate in their answers.

- Each passage about a Guinness World Record holder is followed by questions that target such basic skills as recalling, summarizing, understanding the main idea, making connections, and drawing conclusions.

- Questions progress in difficulty using Bloom's Taxonomy for ease of differentiating instruction and for focused practice on higher level thinking skills, such as predicting, applying, and analyzing.

- Vocabulary questions of various contexts and formats revisit challenging and practical vocabulary words (boldfaced in each passage) by working with words, definitions, and usage.

- Extension activities or critical response questions complete each question page. Students will expand their knowledge and creativity with more than 100 of these bonus questions to choose from.

- Summarizing puzzles and games at the end of each unit monitor student comprehension and reinforce vocabulary with an array of fun and engaging formats.

ARE *YOU* THE NEXT WORLD RECORD-HOLDER?

Do you think that you have what it takes to break a Guinness World Record? You just might! With dedication, persistence, and an idea, anything is possible. If you have an idea and you are ready to commit, get your family's permission and then go for it! Who knows? Your name could be in next year's record book. How do you do it? Read on!

First, what kind of record would you like to break? Do you have a unique talent? Are you the only person able to do something? If your talent is interesting or exciting, you have a good chance!

Do you own a unique object? Is it the only object of its kind? If it's a record that someone can break, such as owning the cow with the longest horns, then you're on your way. Or, if you think that you're the youngest person to achieve a certain feat, Guinness World Records may be interested. Just make sure that the feat is of international interest and, of course, something that is legal to do at your age!

Are you thinking of being the first at something? That's the hardest record to achieve. "Firsts" have to be important enough to have historic or international significance, such as the First Woman to Walk to the North Pole.

Not sure which record to break? Are you interested in going for a record that is regularly broken? The DJ marathon and various mass participation events are the records broken most often.

When you've decided which record to break, complete the registration form on the Guinness World Records Web site. Then, submit an application. Your application will include your proposal for the record. You'll know in about four weeks if your proposal is accepted. If it is, you are ready to go! Make sure that you follow the guidelines carefully. You'll have to collect and submit evidence of your record. Now, all you have to do is break that record!

Did You Know?
Guinness World Records receives more than 60,000 inquiries every year from potential record-breakers. A total of 40,000 records are in the Guinness database.

SKILLS MATRIX

Page Number	Comprehension Strategies								Vocabulary Development			Higher Order Thinking Skills					
	Recalling	Activating Prior Knowledge	Making Connections	Summarizing	Understanding Main Idea	Monitoring Comprehension	Drawing Conclusions	Determining Fact vs. Opinion	Increasing Vocabulary	Using Context Clues	Word Study	Predicting	Application	Analysis	Synthesis	Evaluation	Critical Response
11	✔		✔		✔	✔	✔		✔	✔			✔	✔			
13	✔	✔	✔			✔			✔				✔			✔	✔
15	✔	✔	✔		✔	✔	✔		✔	✔	✔			✔	✔		
17	✔	✔	✔	✔	✔	✔	✔	✔	✔	✔			✔	✔			
19	✔	✔	✔	✔	✔			✔	✔					✔		✔	
21	✔	✔	✔			✔			✔	✔		✔	✔				
23	✔	✔	✔		✔	✔	✔		✔	✔			✔	✔	✔		
25	✔		✔		✔	✔		✔	✔				✔	✔			
27	✔	✔	✔	✔	✔				✔	✔			✔				
29	✔	✔	✔		✔	✔			✔		✔	✔	✔				
31	✔	✔	✔						✔	✔	✔	✔	✔				
33	✔	✔	✔		✔	✔			✔	✔			✔	✔			
35	✔	✔			✔	✔			✔	✔	✔	✔	✔	✔			
36						✔											
37	✔					✔			✔								
39	✔	✔	✔		✔	✔	✔		✔	✔			✔	✔	✔		
41	✔	✔	✔		✔	✔			✔			✔	✔				
43	✔	✔	✔		✔	✔	✔		✔	✔			✔	✔	✔		
45	✔			✔	✔	✔	✔		✔	✔			✔				
47	✔	✔	✔		✔	✔			✔	✔	✔		✔	✔			
49	✔	✔	✔		✔	✔			✔		✔		✔	✔			
51	✔	✔	✔			✔	✔		✔	✔			✔				
53	✔	✔	✔		✔	✔		✔	✔	✔	✔		✔	✔	✔		
55	✔	✔	✔		✔	✔	✔		✔	✔		✔	✔	✔			
57	✔	✔	✔		✔	✔			✔	✔			✔	✔	✔		
58	✔								✔								
59	✔					✔			✔								
61	✔	✔	✔	✔	✔	✔		✔	✔	✔			✔	✔	✔		
63	✔		✔	✔	✔	✔	✔		✔				✔	✔	✔		
65	✔		✔		✔	✔			✔			✔	✔	✔	✔		
67	✔	✔	✔		✔	✔	✔		✔				✔	✔	✔		
69	✔		✔		✔	✔			✔	✔			✔				

PETITE POOCH

■ Read the passage.
Smallest Dog Living (Height), May 12, 2007

Do good things really come in small packages? Lana Elswick (USA) would know. Her dog Boo Boo holds the Guinness World Records™ record for the smallest dog by height. Little Boo Boo is a female, long-haired Chihuahua who lives with Elswick in Raceland, Kentucky.

Chihuahuas are part of the toy group breed of dogs and are typically tiny. They normally range from 6–8 inches (15–20 cm) tall and weigh about 2–6 pounds (1–3 kg). But, this record-setting doggie is exceptionally small. From the tip of her toes to her shoulders, Boo Boo is 4 inches (10 cm) tall. That's a little taller than a coffee mug. Boo Boo weighs 1.5 pounds (680 g).

Elswick says that when Boo Boo was born she was about the size of Elswick's thumb. She was so tiny that she had to be fed with an eyedropper!

Even though Chihuahuas are small, they are typically not timid dogs. They are compared to terriers and have a reputation for having big **egos**. This record-setting Chihuahua is no different. Elswick says Boo Boo has a "big dog attitude." A lot of **spunk** is in that tiny body!

DID YOU KNOW?
The name *Chihuahua* comes from the Mexican state of Chihuahua. Dogs that look like Chihuahuas have been found in ancient paintings in Mexico.

10

Name_____ Date_____

■ Answer the questions.

1. How big was Boo Boo when she was born? _____

_____

2. What breed of dogs are Chihuahuas a part of? _____

_____

3. People who have big **egos** can also be described as:

    A. confident

    B. scared

    C. energetic

    D. talkative

4. Spunk is:

    A. fear

    B. intelligence

    C. beauty

    D. courage

5. Circle *T* for true or *F* for false.

    A. Chihuahua is a state in Mexico.   **T**   **F**

    B. Boo Boo is a wimpy dog.   **T**   **F**

    C. Boo Boo is a short-haired dog.   **T**   **F**

6. Why does the author ask, "Do good things really come in small packages?" at the beginning of the passage? What does this mean? Do you think that good things come in small packages?

_____

_____

■ Choose one extension activity.

A. Drawings of dogs that look like Chihuahuas have been found in ancient paintings in Mexico. Draw a picture of what one of these paintings might look like.

B. Chihuahuas are typically small dogs. Research other breeds of dogs that are normally small. How do they compare in size to Boo Boo?

DIG THIS: WORLD'S LONGEST MASTODON TUSK

■ Read the passage.

Longest Mastodon Tusk, July 28, 2007

This record-breaker is more than two million years old! It is the world's Longest **Mastodon** Tusk. Mastodons were prehistoric mammals. They were related to mammoths and resembled elephants. Scientists are still trying to understand why mastodons became **extinct**. They are hoping that this tusk will give them some clues.

The tusk is 16.5 feet (5 m) long. It was discovered in 2007 by a group of scientists in Greece. Along with the tusk, the group found parts of the animal's jaws and leg bones. They were able to tell that he was a 25- to 30-year-old male. He was probably about 11.5 feet (3.5 m) tall and weighed around 6 tons (5 metric tons). That's the weight of three average-sized cars!

Scientists believe mastodons probably used their tusks to help them do two things: get food and fight. The tusks helped them take down small trees and bend branches to get leaves and twigs. Mastodons also used their tusks to protect themselves against predators and to defend their territory.

DID YOU KNOW?

A mastodon's tusks have rings inside like a tree trunk. These rings give us clues about the animal. Wide rings tell us that the mastodon was eating well and growing fast. Thin rings mean that the animal was growing slowly.

Name_____ Date_____

■ Answer the questions.

1. What is a **mastodon**?_____

_____

2. What two things did mastodons use their tusks for? _____

_____

3. The rings on mastodons' tusks can tell scientists
  A. if they were eating well.
  B. how old they were.
  C. if they had babies.
  D. what they looked like.

4. Circle *T* for true or *F* for false.

  A. The longest tusk belonged to a male mastodon.   T   F

  B. Scientists also uncovered the animal's foot bone in the dig.   T   F

  C. Mastodons ate leaves.   T   F

5. What does it mean to be **extinct**? Name another animal that is extinct.

_____

_____

6. The mastodon is related to what other animals? What animal that is alive today does the mastodon resemble? How are they alike?

_____

_____

■ Choose one statement. Then, explain why you agree or disagree.
  A. Digging for fossils is an expensive waste of time.
  B. Learning about the conditions on Earth long ago can help us in modern times.

THE KING OF DOGS

■ Read the passage.
Tallest Dog Living, February 15, 2010

It would not be hard to spot this pooch at the park. Giant George is the Guinness World Records™ record-breaker for Tallest Dog Living. George is a four-year-old gray Great Dane. Great Danes are large dogs that sometimes are called the "king of dogs." Giant George is 43 inches (1 m) tall from the tops of his shoulders to the pads of his paws. (That's how a dog's height is measured.) George weighs a whopping 245 pounds (111 kg). That is the weight of a large man.

David and Christine Nasser take care of George in Tucson, Arizona. He lives like a king. George eats 110 pounds (50 kg) of food every week and sleeps in his own queen-size bed!

George has been a very busy boy. He has been a guest on several TV shows and has appeared in many national magazines. He even has his own Web site and social Internet pages. George has been enjoying life as a celebrity.

DID YOU KNOW?
Great Danes have great hearts. They are popular family pets because of their sweet and gentle personalities. They are friendly, loving dogs and are not usually **aggressive**. They tend to get along well with other dogs, pets, and people.

■ **Answer the questions.**

1. What breed of dog is Giant George? _____
   _____

2. What adjectives are used to describe this breed in the passage?
   _____

3. In what ways does Giant George live like a king?
   _____
   _____

4. How should you measure dogs to get their height?
   _____

5. Circle *T* for true or *F* for false.

   A. Great Danes usually don't get along with other animals.   **T   F**

   B. Giant George has his own bed.   **T   F**

   C. Giant George eats 110 pounds (50 kg) of food every day.   **T   F**

6. An animal that is **aggressive** would <u>not</u> be described as being:
   A. sweet
   B. forceful
   C. violent
   D. hostile

7. Why does the author call George "a very busy boy"?
   _____
   _____

■ **Choose one extension activity.**

   A. Giant George has been on several television shows. Find other dogs that have been on TV.

   B. What do you think it would be like taking care of a dog as big as Giant George? Write a list of the things that you would have to do with a Great Dane, but you wouldn't have to do with a smaller dog.

OFFICER WOOF

■ Read the passage.
Smallest Police Dog, November 7, 2006

Meet Midge, a police employee that does not carry a gun or wear a badge. She cannot drive either. But, she does ride a motorcycle. Midge is a Chihuahua–rat terrier mix. She holds the world record for Smallest Police Dog.

Midge is 11 inches (28 cm) tall and 23 inches (58 cm) long. She is an official law enforcement work dog. She works in Ohio with her owner, Sheriff Dan McClelland.

Midge passed her certification and became official in November 2006. She works as a narcotics dog. That means she can sniff out marijuana and other drugs.

Most police dogs are larger dogs, like German shepherds and Labrador retrievers. Sometimes suspects complain about large dogs damaging their cars or homes. The fact that Midge is small is an **asset**. She is not likely to damage anything. Also, she can get into small spaces easily and search for illegal drugs.

Midge has a very busy schedule. She goes to daily meetings and out on calls with Sheriff McClelland. When she rides on the sheriff's motorcycle, Midge has her own pair of goggles to wear. She participates in search demonstrations and helps with public anti-drug messages. She helps with arrests, searches, and drug seizures. Midge is very popular. She was even the grand marshal for a Memorial Day parade!

Name_____ Date_____

■ Answer the questions.

1. What is Midge's job? _____
_____

2. Who does Midge work with? _____
_____

3. Another word for **asset** is:
  A. benefit
  B. decrease
  C. negative
  D. attractive

4. Circle *F* for fact or *O* for opinion.

  A. Midge is a great dog.   **F**   **O**

  B. Midge was the grand marshal in a parade.   **F**   **O**

  C. Midge wears goggles when she rides a motorcycle.   **F**   **O**

5. Consider Midge's job duties. What are the benefits of her size? What are the
    possible disadvantages?

  _____

  _____

  _____

6. Midge stays very busy. Do you think that she enjoys her work? Why?

  _____

  _____

■ Choose one extension activity.
  A. Research other dogs in Midge's "profession." What
    additional tasks do they do?
  B. Imagine that you are writing a mystery novel. Write a
    chapter about Midge working to help crack the case.

A BIG OX

■ Read the passage.
Tallest Ox (Ever), November 8, 2007

Meet Fiorino. He holds the Guinness World Records™ record for Tallest Ox. Oxen are like cows, but they work on farms pulling loads instead of giving milk. Fiorino lives in Italy with Antonio Sola. This ox measures 6 feet 8 inches (2.05 m) to the **withers**. That is about as tall as the average professional basketball player!

The ridge between the shoulder blades of a four-legged animal is called the withers. It is usually the tallest point of the animal's body. That is why it is used to measure the height of an animal.

Fiorino is a Chianina ox. This is the largest living breed of cattle in the world. Many people believe Chianina oxen were around long ago, even during ancient Roman times. Chianina oxen were once considered working animals. Farmers put the oxen's strength to work pulling plows or carts. With the invention of farming equipment, like tractors, this breed is now used to produce meat.

DID YOU KNOW?

Oxen are great work animals. The obvious reason is because they are so strong. However, some animals that are strong are not necessarily easy to handle. Oxen possess another important quality that makes them valuable work animals. They are typically very calm, which means they are easy to work with.

Name_____ Date_____

■ Answer the questions.

1. What kind of animal is Fiorino? _____
   _____

2. These animals probably have been around since _____ times.

3. What is an animal's **withers**?
   - **A.** the top of an animal's head
   - **B.** the ridge between the shoulder blades of a four-legged animal
   - **C.** a four-legged animal's legs
   - **D.** an animal's waistline

4. Circle *T* for true or *F* for false.

   A. Fiorino lives in Italy.   T   F

   B. Chianina oxen are not raised to be used as food.   T   F

   C. Fiorino is as tall as the average professional basketball player.   T   F

5. Circle *F* for fact or *O* for opinion.

   A. Fiorino is adorable.   F   O

   B. Antonio Sola is very proud of Fiorino.   F   O

   C. Fiorino's height is measured to his withers.   F   O

6. Chianina oxen were used for farmwork before tractors were invented. What do you think are advantages and disadvantages of using farm animals instead of using a machine?

   _____

   _____

   _____

■ Choose one extension activity.

   A. Research other animals that worked on farms before the introduction of modern farming equipment.
   B. Write a limerick about Fiorino and Antonio.

CREEPY CREEPY-CRAWLY

■ Read the passage.
Most Destructive Insect

This bug really bugs people. The record-holder for most destructive insect is the desert locust (*Schistocerca gregaria*). Locusts are related to grasshoppers. Desert locusts live in regions of Africa, the Middle East, and western Asia. These locusts are only about 2 inches (5 cm) long and weigh less than an ounce (28 g). But, do not let their small size fool you. They can cause serious damage.

When the weather is right, locusts gather in huge swarms. In one day, a hungry locust can eat its own weight in food. A small swarm of 50 million locusts can really chow down. In 24 hours, they can eat enough food to **sustain** 500 people for one year.

In 1958, locusts in Ethiopia devoured 151,500 tons (69 metric tons) of grain. It was **devastating**. They destroyed food that would have fed a million people for a whole year. Farmers attempt to scare locusts away by making noise, digging trenches, or setting traps. The method that is most often used is spraying chemicals. Desert locusts are very difficult to control.

DID YOU KNOW?
In Southeast Asia, people eat grilled locusts stuffed with peanuts.

Name_____ Date_____

■ Answer the questions.

1. Where do desert locusts live? _____

_____

2. How much can one locust eat in one day? _____

_____

3. Use the word **sustain** in a sentence. _____

_____

4. Devastating means:

    A. destructive

    B. ugly

    C. rebirth

    D. cold

5. Circle *T* for true or *F* for false.

    A. Grasshoppers are the most destructive insects.   **T**   **F**

    B. Some people eat locusts.   **T**   **F**

    C. The desert locust is a huge bug.   **T**   **F**

6. A small swarm of locusts can eat enough in one day to sustain 500 people for a year. Think of possible ways that people could protect their food and crops from swarms of locusts.

_____

_____

_____

■ Choose one extension activity.

    A. In 1958, swarms of locusts caused devastation in Ethiopia. Research other times in history where locusts had a widespread effect.

    B. Create a recipe using locusts as an ingredient. Write your recipe.

21

GUINEA-POTAMUS?

■ Read the passage.
Largest Rodent

What looks like a cross between a hippopotamus and a guinea pig? Answer: a capybara. Capybaras (*Hydrochoerus hydrochaeris*) hold the world record for largest rodents. Adult capybaras can be more than 4 feet (122 cm) long and 1.5 feet (46 cm) tall. They can weigh more than 100 pounds (45 kg).

Capybaras are from Central and South America. They live in the swamplands. This is the perfect place for them because they love water. Capybaras can stay underwater for up to five minutes. They can even sleep underwater with their noses sticking out for air!

Capybara means "master of grasses." They are **herbivores** that eat mostly grasses and aquatic plants. They are known for being calm animals. Capybaras are very vocal. They communicate by whimpering, clicking, purring, and barking.

DID YOU KNOW?
Some people keep capybaras as pets. They are smart animals. One blind man trained his pet capybara to be his guide animal.

Name_____ Date_____

■ Answer the questions.

1. Where are capybaras from?_____

2. How does a capybara communicate? _____

_____

3. What are **herbivores**?

    A. animals that eat herbs

    B. animals that eat only plants

    C. animals that eat meat

    D. animals that sleep during the day

4. Circle *T* for true or *F* for false.

    A. Capybaras live in the desert.   T   F

    B. Some people keep capybaras as pets.   T   F

    C. Capybaras do not like water.   T   F

5. What does *capybara* mean? Why do you think that the animal has this name?

_____

_____

6. The capybara is a rodent. Compare it to other rodents that you know about. What are the similarities? What are the differences?

_____

_____

_____

■ Choose one extension activity.

A. Some people keep capybaras as pets. What do you think it would be like to have a capybara as a pet? What would you name your capybara? Write a diary entry of a typical day spent with your pet capybara.

B. Research other animals that are from the same regions as capybaras. Which animals live in the same environment as the capybara?

HUMPTY DEPUTY

■ Read the passage.
Highest-Ranking Camel, April 5, 2003

Have you ever met a deputy sheriff who spits and has a hump? Then, you probably haven't met the world's Highest-Ranking Camel. Deputy Bert is a reserve deputy sheriff for the Los Angeles County Sheriff's Department in San Dimas, California. He regularly goes on patrol with his trainer, Nance Fite.

Bert was born in 1997. He is about seven feet (2 m) tall and weighs 1,800 pounds (3,900 kg). He is a **dromedary** camel. That means he has one hump.

Bert works with Fite in the community. He is very **genial**. He attends events and participates in parades. He and Fite promote safety and encourage people to stay off drugs. Bert likes meeting children. He smells their hair. (That means "hello" in the camel world.) Bert always checks out their hands too, hoping to find treats.

Bert has a big appetite. He eats about 20 pounds (9 kg) of hay every day. Some people may consider Deputy Bert a famous celebrity. He has appeared in movies, TV shows, and documentaries.

DID YOU KNOW?
If camels feel threatened by something, they will spit on it. The spit is not typical spit. It is made of vomit and saliva. In other words, don't mess with Deputy Bert!

Name_____ Date_____

■ Answer the questions.

1. What is Bert's work title? _____

2. What are Bert's duties?_____

_____

_____

3. What is a **dromedary** camel?

    A. a famous animal

    B. an animal with two sets of teeth

    C. a camel with a small hump

    D. a camel with one hump

4. Someone who is **genial** would <u>not</u> be described as:

    A. friendly

    B. uncomfortable

    C. happy

    D. social

5. Circle *F* for fact or *O* for opinion.

    A. Children love camels.   F   O

    B. Bert eats about 20 pounds (9 kg) of hay every day.   F   O

    C. Bert works in California.   F   O

6. Bert and Fite talk about safety and anti-drug messages. How do you think Bert helps with these topics? Do you imagine that Bert does a good job?

_____

_____

_____

_____

■ Choose one extension activity.

A. Research other animals that have helped police do their work.

B. Cartoons are funny drawings that are meant to make people laugh or look at something in a new way. Draw a cartoon of Deputy Bert working in California.

ONE OF A KIND

■ Read the passage.

Most Endangered Animal

George is called Lonesome George for good reason. He is the last member of a subspecies of Galápagos giant tortoises. That makes him the rarest creature alive.

George lives at the Charles Darwin Research Station on the island of Santa Cruz in the Galápagos Islands. He weighs about 200 pounds (91 kg) and is 40 inches (102 cm) long. No one knows exactly how old he is. Scientists estimate that he is between 70 and 80 years old. His age may seem amazing, but that is not old for tortoises. They can live to be almost 200 years old.

Giant tortoises are herbivores. George loves to eat plants. George lives a comfortable life at the research station. He shares a pen with two female tortoises from the island of Isabela. He likes his "me time" and hangs out alone in shrubs. He also has a pool to use when he feels like taking a dip.

How did this subspecies of Galápagos giant tortoises become almost extinct? Sailors and fishermen hunted them for their meat. Goats also contributed to their extinction. When large populations of goats were brought onto the island, they ate away at the tortoises' **habitat**.

Name_____ Date_____

■ **Answer the questions.**

1. How old is Lonesome George?_____

_____

2. What has caused the near extinction of Lonesome George's subspecies of

Galápagos tortoises? _____

_____

3. What is a tortoise's **habitat**?

    A. a tortoise's diet

    B. a tortoise's habits

    C. a tortoise's shell

    D. a tortoise's place to live

4. Circle *T* for true or *F* for false.

    A. George lives on the island of Isabela.   **T**   **F**

    B. George eats meat.   **T**   **F**

    C. Tortoises can live up to 200 years.   **T**   **F**

5. Why do you think that he is called Lonesome George? _____

_____

_____

6. Lonesome George is the Most Endangered Animal. Can you think of ways that scientists might have prevented this situation?

_____

_____

■ **Choose one extension activity.**

A. Lonesome George lives in the Galápagos Islands. Research other animals on these islands.

B. Write a poem for George for his next birthday.

RECORD-BREAKING MONSTER

■ Read the passage.
Most Dangerous Lizard

Are you ready to meet a real monster? The Gila (HEE-la) monster is a large lizard that lives in the **arid** parts of Mexico and the southwestern United States. These lizards are covered in scales that look like brightly colored beads. They can grow to be 24 inches (60 cm) long. The Gila monster holds the world record for Most Dangerous Lizard.

Gila monsters are **venomous**. Venomous animals inject poison by biting or stinging their victims. The Gila monster bites its victim. Small grooves in the lizard's teeth help the venom seep into the wound. Gila monsters have extremely strong teeth. They may hang on as they bite and chew to get the venom to go deeper into the wound. A Gila monster carries enough venom to kill two people!

Gila monsters do not go around looking for victims. They tend to avoid humans and other large animals. Gila monsters attack only when someone or something disturbs them.

DID YOU KNOW?
Diabetes is a serious medical condition that affects about 7 percent of all Americans. The U.S. Food and Drug Administration approved a drug for diabetes made with parts of the Gila monster's saliva. Some people call the drug *lizard spit*.

Carson-Dellosa

Name_____ Date_____

■ Answer the questions.

1. What is a Gila monster? _____

_____

2. How much venom does a Gila monster carry?_____

_____

3. An antonym for **arid** is:

    A. dry

    B. moist

    C. grassy

    D. forest

4. What does the word **venomous** mean? What other animals can you think of that are venomous?

_____

_____

5. Circle *T* for true or *F* for false.

    A. Gila monsters are friendly.   **T**   **F**

    B. Gila monsters are covered in scales that look like beads.   **T**   **F**

    C. Gila monsters have strong teeth.   **T**   **F**

6. If you came near a Gila monster, what do you think would be the best way to handle the situation?

_____

_____

■ Choose one extension activity.

A. A helpful drug was created using parts of the Gila monster's saliva. Research other remedies that include animal products.

B. Imagine you are the first person to ever see a Gila monster. Write a journal entry about your encounter with this dangerous lizard.

MING THE CLAM

■ Read the passage.

Longest-Living Animal, October 28, 2007

The Longest-Living Animal is a quahog clam. Ming the Clam was found off the north coast of Iceland. It was between 405 and 410 years old. The clam was named after the Ming dynasty, the Chinese family that ruled China when Ming the Clam was born.

Researchers from Bangor University in the United Kingdom found Ming the Clam in 2006. They studied the growth rings in the shell. That is how they determine how old a clam is.

Quahog clams are known for their **longevity**. Scientists do not know why they age so slowly. They hope that studying these clams will lead to discoveries about the aging process.

The rings tell scientists more than the clam's age. They reveal a lot about the environment that the clam lived in, and they help scientists understand environmental changes. For example, scientists can learn what temperature the water was by looking at the rings. They can also determine what the clam was eating. One scientist calls these clams "tiny tape recorders" because of all the information that they hold.

Name_____ Date_____

■ **Answer the questions.**

1. Where was Ming found?_____
_____

2. Why is this clam named *Ming*?_____
_____

3. What does **longevity** mean?

    A. small

    B. long life

    C. ability to dig

    D. short break

4. Circle *T* for true or *F* for false.

    A. Researchers from China found Ming.   T   F

    B. Scientists can learn about the environment that a clam
    lived in from its shell.   T   F

    C. Ming was over 400 years old.   T   F

5. A metaphor compares two unlike things. What metaphor did one scientist use to describe clams?
_____
_____

6. Researchers estimated Ming's age by looking at the rings in the shell. What other living things have growth rings that share information?
_____
_____

■ **Choose one extension activity.**

A. Research events that occurred in your country's history at the time of Ming's birth. Write a journal entry about something that was going on about that time.

B. Scientists are hoping to discover information about the aging process through researching clamshells. What might scientists learn about aging?

THE PIG THAT FLEW

■ Read the passage.
Highest Jump by a Pig, August 22, 2004

Have you heard the phrase "when pigs fly"? This is a pig that practically did! Kotetsu, a potbellied pig, jumped 27.5 inches (70 cm) into the air. That makes Kotetsu the highest-jumping pig in the world. Kotetsu performed his extraordinary leap in August of 2004 in Japan.

Many people keep potbellied pigs as pets. They are very smart animals. Potbellied pigs are friendly and playful. They love attention. They can be housebroken, taught to walk on a leash, and even taught to perform tricks!

Most potbellied pigs weigh around 150 pounds (67 kg). They are 14–18 inches (35–45 cm) from the bottom of their hooves to the top of their shoulders. Potbellied pigs are **omnivores**, which means that they eat plants and meat. Potbellied pigs especially like grass, eggs, and fish.

DID YOU KNOW?
When the Chinese calendar was created more than 3,000 years ago, a different animal was assigned to each year. The pig represents **prosperity**. Some people think that this symbol led to the idea of a piggy bank.

Name_____ Date_____

■ **Answer the questions.**

1. How did Kotetsu earn a world record? _____
_____

2. What are some personality traits of a potbellied pig? _____
_____
_____

3. What are **omnivores**? What are some animals that are omnivores?_____
_____
_____

4. Another word for **prosperity** is:
   A. luck
   B. success
   C. intelligence
   D. honesty

5. Circle *T* for true or *F* for false.

   A. Potbellied pigs make great pets.   T   F

   B. Kotetsu jumped in Japan.   T   F

   C. Potbellied pigs are mean animals.   T   F

6. Do you think Kotetsu likes jumping? Why or why not?
_____
_____

■ **Choose one extension activity.**
A. The pig represents one of the years in the Chinese calendar.
   Research the Chinese calendar to learn the other animals
   on it and what each represents.
B. Draw a Venn diagram comparing a potbellied pig
   with another mammal of your choice.

33

STICK OUT YOUR TONGUE

■ Read the passage.
Longest Tongue—Dog, 2002

Brandy has this record licked. She holds the world record for longest dog tongue. Her tongue is 17 inches (43 cm) long. Brandy is a tan and white boxer. She lives with her owner, John Scheid, in Michigan.

Scheid says that Brandy was a very happy and perfectly healthy puppy. Brandy was born with her **elongated** licker. Scheid made a **prediction** that Brandy would grow into her tongue. But, as Brandy continued to grow, so did her incredible tongue.

Brandy is more than a world record-holder. She has numerous awards. She won first place in an ugly dog contest sponsored by a television network in 1999. She received second place in Stupid Pet Tricks in 2000. Brandy even received second place in an owner-pet look-alike contest in 2001. How do you think John Scheid feels about that?

One of Brandy's best tricks is eating from a bowl 13 inches (33 cm) away. It is best to stand back when she eats. Her giant tongue doesn't make things neat, and bits of food fly everywhere.

Brandy has many fans. She has appeared on television and has her own fan club and her own Web site.

Name_____ Date_____

■ **Answer the questions.**

1. Who is Brandy? _____
   _____

2. What is an antonym for **elongated**?
   A. slippery
   B. wet
   C. shortened
   D. lengthened

3. What is a **prediction**?
   A. an opinion
   B. the way a person tells a joke
   C. a person's biggest dream
   D. what someone thinks will happen

4. What other awards has Brandy received? Which contest would be the most fun for you to watch? Why?
   _____
   _____

5. Brandy's long tongue can get in the way of eating and can make a mess. What other things do you think would be different for Brandy because of her tongue?
   _____
   _____

6. The author asks how Scheid might feel about one of Brandy's awards. Which one is it? How do you think Scheid feels about it?
   _____
   _____
   _____

■ **Choose one extension activity.**

A. Draw a picture of Brandy in action with her lengthy tongue.
B. Research this breed of dogs. Share five interesting facts with your classmates or family.

REVIEW: AMAZING ANIMALS

■ Ready to crack the code?

First, unscramble the record-holders' names. Then, copy the letters into the corresponding numbered squares to crack the code and read the secret message. Some of the letters are already filled in.

1	2		3	4	5		6	7	8		9	10	11	12		13	14	15		16	17
			C				–		A					A				A			

RECORD-HOLDERS' NAMES:

MENLOEOS GEOGER __ **O** __ **E** **S** __ __ __ __ __ __ __ __ __
16   11   15   12

OBBOOO __ __ __ __ __ __
6

ITANG REGGOE **G** __ __ __ __ __ __ __ __ __ __
14   13   1

MIEGD __ __ __ __ __
5   2

NOIRIOF __ __ __ __ __ __ __
7

TERB __ __ __ __
8

IGMN __ __ __ __
10

SUTKOTE __ __ __ __ __ __ __
9 3   17

RYDBAN __ __ __ **N** __ __
4

REVIEW: AMAZING ANIMALS

■ Use the clues to complete the puzzle.

ACROSS

2. Strengthen or support physically
3. A type of camel with one hump
5. Used to describe a Gila monster
7. Part of the reptile George's name
9. This dog has spunk.
10. Quahog clams are known for this.

DOWN

1. Giant rodent
4. Prehistoric mammal similar to elephants
6. Loves veggies
8. Smallest Police Dog

SKY-HIGH DOOR

■ Read the passage.
Largest Door

Imagine walking through a door as big as a skyscraper. Each of the four doors on the NASA Vehicle Assembly Building (VAB) is that big! These doors are the largest in the world.

The VAB is at NASA's Kennedy Space Center in Florida. Each door is 460 feet (140 m) high. That is as tall as a 35-story building. Completely opening or closing each door takes 45 minutes.

The VAB originally was built for assembling the *Saturn* and *Apollo* rockets. The doors had to be big enough to let the rockets pass through. Now, the building is used for space shuttle operations.

The NASA Vehicle Assembly Building is the largest one-story building in the world. It is even taller than the Statue of Liberty!

DID YOU KNOW?
The inside of the NASA Vehicle Assembly Building is so **enormous** that it has its own weather. Rain clouds form below the ceiling on very humid days. But, it has never actually rained inside the building.

Name_____ Date_____

■ Answer the questions.

1. How many doors hold the world record for Largest Door?_____

2. How tall are the doors? _____

   _____

3. An antonym for **enormous** is:
   A. small
   B. medium
   C. gigantic
   D. silly

4. Circle *T* for true or *F* for false.

   A. A 30-story building can fit through the door of the VAB.   T   F

   B. It takes two hours to open one of the doors.   T   F

   C. The VAB is used for space shuttle operations.   T   F

5. Why are the doors of the VAB so big? Could smaller doors have been used for this building?

   _____

   _____

   _____

6. Why does the building have its own weather?

   _____

   _____

■ Choose one extension activity.

A. The building was originally made for the *Apollo* and *Saturn* rockets.
   Research these rockets. What were their missions?
B. Imagine that you are a NASA employee working on a rocket in the
   VAB. Write a journal entry about your typical workday.

TOWERING TEEN

■ Read the passage.
Tallest Girl, January 16, 2009

Malee Duangdee (Thailand) certainly stands out in a crowd. At 6 feet 10 inches (208 cm), she is the world's Tallest Girl under 18 years old. The average height of a woman from her country is less than 5 feet 2 inches (157 cm).

Duangdee's amazing **stature** is caused by a health condition. She has a tumor on her pituitary gland. The tumor makes her body produce too much growth hormone. When she was four years old, she was as tall as a seven-year-old. She was growing much faster than other children and needed new shoes almost every month. By the time that she was 10 years old, Duangdee was 6 feet tall (1.8 m). At age 12, she was 6 feet 2 inches (1.9 m)—nearly a foot taller than her dad.

Duangdee had to stop going to school because she didn't fit on her father's tiny motorbike. But, Duangdee likes her title as tallest girl. She enjoys her fame and her Guinness World Records™ record.

DID YOU KNOW?
You are taller in the morning than you are at night. During the night, you usually lie down. During the day, you are mostly upright. When you are upright, gravity pulls you down. So, as the day goes on, gravity shrinks your body just a little.

Name_____ Date_____

■ Answer the questions.

1. What is the average height of a woman in Thailand?_____

_____

2. How tall was Duangdee when she was 10 years old?_____

_____

3. Stature means:

    A. model

    B. heavy

    C. height

    D. large

4. Circle *T* for true or *F* for false.

    A. Duangdee had to get new shoes every week when she was a child.   **T**   **F**

    B. Duangdee is in perfect health.   **T**   **F**

    C. Duangdee enjoys her fame.   **T**   **F**

5. Why did Duangdee have to stop going to school? What are some solutions that might help Duangdee continue her education?

_____

_____

_____

6. When she was four years old, Duangdee says that she was as tall as a seven-year-old. What would have been some positives and negatives for Duangdee at that age and size?

_____

_____

_____

■ Choose one extension activity.

A. Research the pituitary gland and write an explanation of its function in the body.

B. Being as tall as Duangdee must make life very different. Write a list of things that would be easier to do if you were that tall.

LOUD AND CLEAR

■ Read the passage.

Largest Awareness Ribbon Made of Flowers, November 16, 2007

Awareness ribbons can be worn to remind people about a cause. Although this record-breaking ribbon cannot actually be worn, it is a big reminder. Dubai Healthcare City, in the country of Dubai, created the world's Largest Awareness Ribbon Made of Flowers. About 105,000 pink carnations formed the ribbon shape. It measured more than 95 feet (29 m) long.

The pink ribbon stands for breast cancer. Dubai Healthcare City wanted to raise awareness of this disease. Its focus was early detection. When cancer is spotted early, survival rates soar. Most people with breast cancer in Arab countries do not seek assistance early. Dubai Healthcare City wants to change that.

The ribbon was in Zabeel Park in Dubai. A walkathon to raise money followed the **unveiling**. About 2,500 people participated in the walk. The money that was raised was used for local cancer research.

DID YOU KNOW?
The color of an awareness ribbon stands for its cause. Groups use ribbons to show support or to raise awareness. Some causes share colors.

Name_____ Date_____

■ **Answer the questions.**

1. What was the giant awareness ribbon made of? _____

2. What other event took place at the park that day? _____
   _____

3. A walkathon to raise money followed the **unveiling**. What was the unveiling?
   _____

4. Why do people make awareness ribbons? Have you or someone you know worn an awareness ribbon? What was it for?
   _____
   _____
   _____

5. Do you think that the giant ribbon did what the creators wanted it to do? Why or why not?
   _____
   _____
   _____

■ **Choose one extension activity.**

A. What is a cause that is important to you? Describe different ways that you could raise awareness for your cause. What would your awareness ribbon look like?

B. Research different awareness ribbons and learn what their colors stand for.

A LIFE-SAVING TRANSPLANT

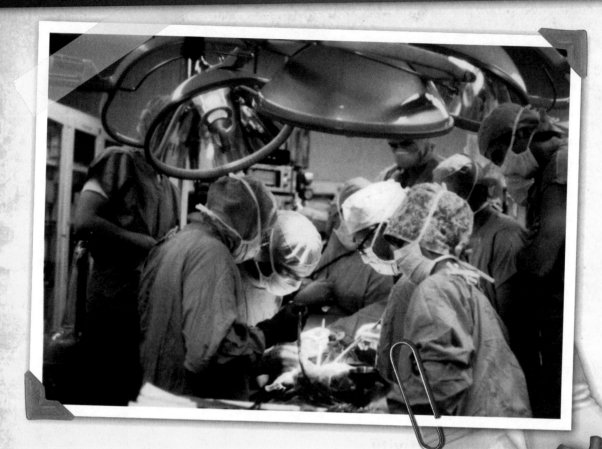

■ Read the passage.
Earliest Heart-Lung Transplant, 1981

Doctor Bruce Reitz (USA) performed the Earliest Heart-Lung **Transplant** in 1981 at Stanford Medical Center in California. A heart-lung transplant is a type of surgery that replaces a person's heart and lungs.

The heart pumps blood through the body. It works hard. Every day, it pumps about 2,000 gallons (7,600 L) of blood. It beats about 100,000 times a day.

People have two lungs. They are in the rib cage on either side of the heart. The lungs help with breathing. They bring oxygen into the blood and push carbon dioxide out.

When Dr. Reitz performed the surgery, he had a team of doctors working with him. They had spent years experimenting and researching before the transplant. **Donor** organs were transplanted into the patient. A heart-lung transplant is still a very rare operation. Only about 100 are performed each year in the United States.

Name_____ Date_____

■ Answer the questions.

1. What is a heart-lung transplant?_____

_____

2. What is the function of the lungs?_____

_____

_____

3. During a **transplant**, something is
   A. repaired.
   B. moved from one place to another.
   C. cleaned.
   D. examined.

4. A **donor** organ is:
   A. an organ given by someone else
   B. an organ grown in a lab
   C. an extra organ
   D. a damaged organ

5. Circle *T* for true or *F* for false.

   A. The first heart-lung transplant was performed in 1981.   T   F

   B. The human body has one lung.   T   F

   C. The heart brings oxygen to the blood.   T   F

6. Why do you think that a heart-lung transplant is a rare operation?

_____

_____

■ Choose one extension activity.

A. Research organ transplants. What other organs have been transplanted successfully?

B. Imagine that you were a TV reporter in 1981. Write the news report that you would give about this surgery.

WALKING ON AIR

■ Read the passage.

Longest Bridge, Suspension Bridge for Pedestrians, October 30, 2006

Suspension bridges are the longest bridges in the world. The Guinness World Records™ record-holder for Longest Suspension Bridge for **Pedestrians** is the Kokonoe Yume. This bridge is in Kokonoe, Japan. It is 1,280 feet (390 m) long and 568 feet (173 m) high.

The name *Yume* means dreams. From the bridge, people can see **dramatic** views of cliffs, waterfalls, and the Naruko-gawa Gorge. It takes about 13 minutes to walk across the Kokonoe Yume Bridge.

Kokonoe Yume has a narrow walkway. It is 5 feet (1.5 m) wide. Suspension bridges are flexible, so they move gently in the wind. Walking across a bridge like Kokonoe can make a person feel dizzy. Some pedestrians find it scary, and others find it exciting.

DID YOU KNOW?

A suspension bridge is a hanging bridge. It suspends from huge cables that run from one end to the other. The cables are suspended between towers.

46

Name_____ Date_____

■ Answer the questions.

1. What can a person see from the Kokonoe Yume bridge? _____

_____

2. Where is the Kokonoe Yume bridge? _____

_____

3. An antonym for the word **dramatic** is:

    A. boring

    B. beautiful

    C. spectacular

    D. automatic

4. If people are **pedestrians**, they are

    A. foot doctors.

    B. people who walk.

    C. people who ride bikes.

    D. horseback riders.

5. What does the word *Yume* mean in English? Why do you think that the bridge was given that name?

_____

_____

_____

6. Some people find walking across a suspension bridge scary, and some find it thrilling. Why would a person find it scary? Why would he find it thrilling?

_____

_____

_____

■ Choose one extension activity.

A. The Kokonoe Yume is a suspension bridge. Research other suspension bridges. Where are they located? How long are they?

B. Imagine that you are on the Kokonoe Yume. Write a poem about your experience as you walk across the bridge.

BUGGED

■ Read the passage.
Highest Frequency of Ultrasound Produced by an Arthropod, November 2007

If you are waiting to hear the sounds of a male Arachnoscelis (ah-RACK-no-SELL-is), prepare to wait a long time. This insect makes a sound higher than a person can hear. These sounds are called **ultrasounds**. The male Arachnoscelis holds the record for highest frequency ultrasound of any known **arthropod**. Frequency describes how a sound pitch is measured. When the pitch is high, the frequency is high.

Humans cannot hear sounds above 20 kilohertz. An Arachnoscelis makes a sound measured at 130 kilohertz.

An Arachnoscelis is a katydid. It is in the same family as grasshoppers and crickets. These katydids live in the tropical rain forests of Colombia, South America.

Scientists have learned how an Arachnoscelis creates ultrasounds. A "scraper" is on the right wing of the insect. After the insect rubs its wings together, the "scraper" springs back and makes the sound.

DID YOU KNOW?
Many other creatures make sounds that we cannot hear. Dolphins, bats, and mice also produce ultrasounds.

48

Name_____ Date_____

■ Answer the questions.

1. What is the highest measured sound that a human can hear? _____

_____

2. What insects are in the same family as the Arachnoscelis?_____

_____

3. What are **ultrasounds**?_____

_____

4. Circle *T* for true or *F* for false.

    A. The Arachnoscelis lives in tropical rain forests.   T   F

    B. A person can hear every sound that a dolphin makes.   T   F

    C. The Arachnoscelis is a katydid.   T   F

5. An Arachnoscelis makes an ultrasound by:
    A. using a "scraper" on its wing.
    B. using a "scraper" on its legs.
    C. spitting.
    D. chewing food.

6. The Arachnoscelis holds the world record for highest frequency ultrasound of any known **arthropod**. Look up *arthropod* and write its definition. List other examples of arthropods.

_____

_____

_____

_____

_____

■ Choose one extension activity.
    A. Research other animals and insects that live in the same habitat as the Arachnoscelis.
    B. Create a picture booklet of animals and insects that make ultrasounds.

TERRIFIC TANK

■ Read the passage.
Largest Aquarium, November 2005

This place blows all others out of the water. The Georgia Aquarium holds the Guinness World Records™ record for Largest Aquarium. It is in Atlanta, Georgia. The aquarium holds 8 million gallons (30 million L) of water. It would take more than 13 Olympic swimming pools to hold all that water.

The aquarium opened in 2005. It is so huge that 230 average-sized American homes could fit inside! The outside of the building is unique. It is made of blue metal and glass. It looks like a ship coming through a wave.

About 120,000 fish and animals live in the aquarium. Whale sharks, beluga whales, and manta rays are the most famous **residents**.

The biggest area in this aquarium is a 6.3 million gallon (24 million L) tank. It holds whale sharks. Whale sharks are the largest fish in the world, and the aquarium is proud to have them. The whole building was designed around the whale shark exhibit. The Georgia Aquarium is the only place in the United States where people can see these animals in action.

Name_____ Date_____

■ Answer the questions.

1. Why is the outside of the Georgia Aquarium unique? _____

_____

2. What size is the whale shark tank? _____

_____

3. Another word for **residents** is:
   A. fish
   B. animals
   C. occupants
   D. relatives

4. Circle *T* for true or *F* for false.

   A. Three aquariums in the United States have whale sharks on display.   T   F

   B. The Georgia Aquarium is in Atlanta.   T   F

   C. Beluga whales live in the aquarium's largest tank.   T   F

5. The Georgia Aquarium was designed around the whale sharks. Why do you think that the aquarium chose to do that?

_____

_____

_____

6. About 120,000 fish and animals live in the Georgia Aquarium. What are the challenges of taking care of so many fish and animals? Have you or anyone you know taken care of a fish or an animal? Explain your experience.

_____

_____

_____

■ Choose one extension activity.
   A. Imagine that you are designing a new aquarium. How would you want it to look? Design the outside and draw it.
   B. Research five facts you did not know about whale sharks.

POPPING PEEPERS

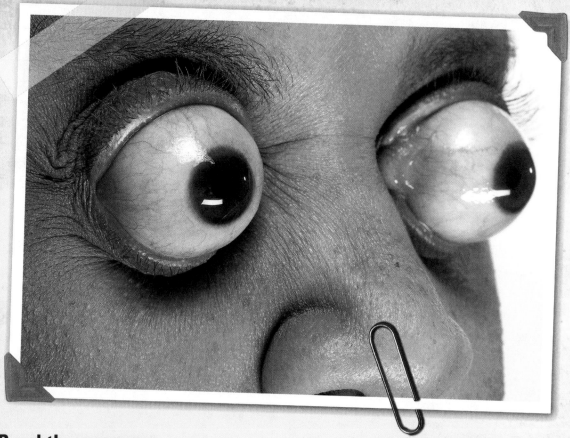

■ Read the passage.
Farthest Eyeball Popper, November 2, 2007

Sometimes when cartoon characters look surprised or **amazed**, their eyes pop right out of their heads. Kim Goodman (USA) is not a cartoon character, but she knows how to look like one. Goodman holds the Guinness World Records™ record for Farthest Eyeball Popper. Goodman can pop her eyes 0.47 inch (12 mm) out of their sockets!

Goodman did not always know that she had popping peepers. One day, she was hit in the head with a hockey mask, and her eyeballs popped out. After discovering her unusual talent, she was able to pop them out whenever she wanted. Sometimes they would pop out when she yawned. Goodman says that she simply squints, pulls her eyelids back, and out they come.

DID YOU KNOW?
Globe luxation is the ability to pop out one's eyes. Doctors do not **recommend** it. It can strain blood vessels and nerves between the eyes and the head.

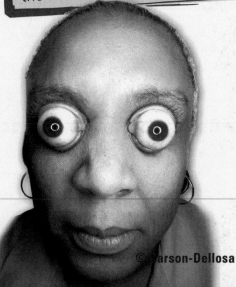

©Carson-Dellosa

Name_____ Date_____

■ Answer the questions.

1. How far can Kim Goodman pop out her eyes?_____

_____

2. Globe luxation is:_____

_____

3. Recommend means:

    A. suggest

    B. improve

    C. damage

    D. strengthen

4. Which word is <u>not</u> a synonym for **amazed**?

    A. surprised

    B. astonished

    C. amused

    D. stunned

5. Circle *F* for fact or *O* for opinion.

    A. Doctors do not recommend that people pop out their eyes.   **F**   **O**

    B. Sometimes Goodman's eyes pop out when she yawns.   **F**   **O**

    C. Goodman can pop her eyes out farther than anyone else in the world.   **F**   **O**

6. How did Goodman discover her hidden talent? Do you have a hidden talent? How did you discover it?

_____

_____

_____

■ Choose one extension activity.

A. Draw a cartoon of an animal popping out his eyes. Draw what he is looking at.

B. Make a list of actions that cartoon characters can do but that an average person cannot.

ROBOT DOG

■ Read the passage.
Farthest Distance Covered by a Quadruped Robot, 2005

Don't expect this dog to bark at your neighbor or lick your face. BigDog isn't a real dog. BigDog is a highly advanced robot. It can walk, run, and climb. Most amazing of all is BigDog's **stamina**. It can go for miles. BigDog set a Guinness World Records™ record for four-legged robots, traveling 12.8 miles (20.6 km) without any aid.

BigDog is powered by a gasoline engine and guided by a computer and a network of sensors. This **quadruped's** legs are specially built to mimic the actions of a real dog. BigDog is 3.28 feet (1 m) long and 2.29 feet (0.7 m) tall. It weighs 165 pounds (75 kg). That makes it about the size of a large dog.

BigDog has a keen sense of balance. On ice, it might start off like a newborn calf, slipping and sliding. But, BigDog will quickly right itself and move on its way. BigDog can plow through deep snow and walk over the roughest terrain. This robot can run nearly 4 miles (6.5 km) an hour and climb a 35-degree slope while carrying a heavy load.

BigDog image courtesy of Boston Dynamics ©2009

BigDog looks kind of silly. Some people say that the robot resembles two people walking as they carry an overturned raft on their heads. But, BigDog is no joke. It was designed to do serious work, like space exploration.

The company that created BigDog is continuing to make improvements to the robot. So, we can look forward to all sorts of new records being set by the next generation of BigDogs!

Name_____ Date_____

■ Answer the questions.

1. According to the passage, BigDog can

    A. swim.

    B. run.

    C. talk.

2. Circle *T* for true or *F* for false.

    A. BigDog set a record for three-legged robots.   T   F

    B. BigDog runs on gasoline.   T   F

    C. BigDog is the size of a small dog.   T   F

3. BigDog would most properly be called a

    A. machine.

    B. toy.

    C. mistake.

4. What is **stamina**? Why is it important for BigDog to have stamina?

_____

_____

5. What is a **quadruped**? Name three other quadrupeds.

_____

_____

6. In what ways would it be easier to care for BigDog than to care for a real dog? In what ways would it be harder?

_____

_____

7. How would you think BigDog might be able to help with space exploration?

_____

_____

■ Choose one extension activity.

A. Is BigDog's appearance important? Why or why not?

B. What do you think the dangers are in relying on robots to perform tasks that humans usually do?

FAR-REACHING FINGERNAILS

■ Read the passage.
Longest Fingernails—Single Hand, February 4, 2004

One look at Shridhar Chillal's (India) hands and you know he's probably not very good at playing the piano. Why? The fingernails on his left hand are the Longest Fingernails in the world. They range in length from 51 inches (130 cm) to 62 inches (157 cm). His left hand displays a total 23 feet (7 m) of fingernails. That's even taller than a full-grown adult giraffe! No one has beaten his Guinness World Records™ record for 20 years.

At 16 years old, Chillal was inspired by a Chinese priest and decided to let the nails on his left hand grow. The priest had let his fingernails grow to 22 inches (56 cm), and Chillal wanted to beat his record. He let the nails on his left hand grow for nearly 50 years. Chillal succeeded by growing his fingernails more than twice as long as the priest's.

After almost 50 years of growth, his long, spiraling nails do not look like fingernails at all. They look more like dark, thick, **gnarled** tree roots. His cinnamon bun–like thumbnail is his longest nail. At a whopping 62 inches (157 cm), it is over 5 feet long (1.5 m).

No one ever said that growing record-breaking fingernails was easy. Chillal has to cover his nails in a special bag to protect them. He constantly worries about them breaking. He even has trouble sleeping because he is so petrified of damaging his hard work. He hasn't had a good night's sleep in almost 50 years! Chillal is fortunate to have a wife who helps him with daily tasks, like brushing his teeth and getting dressed.

Name_____ Date_____

■ Answer the questions.

1. Why did Shridhar Chillal decide to grow his fingernails? _____
_____

2. What does the word **gnarled** mean?
   A. buried
   B. twisted
   C. wet
   D. hollow

3. As of 2010, for how many years has Chillal held his record? _____
_____

4. Chillal prevents his long nails from breaking by
   A. covering them with a bag.
   B. being a light sleeper.
   C. letting his wife assist him with daily tasks.
   D. all of the above.

5. Do you think Chillal is happy about his decision to grow his nails so long? Why or why not?
_____
_____

6. Do you think he could have grown his nails as long without someone's help? Why or why not?
_____
_____

7. Do you think that the author provides enough information to help you understand Chillal's life and personality? If not, what else would you like to know about him?
_____
_____

■ Choose one extension activity.

A. What might be some benefits of having fingernails as long as Chillal's nails?

B. Imagine wearing Chillal's nails for one full day. How would it affect your day? Write a list of all of the things that would be different.

REVIEW: ENGINEERING, SCIENCE & THE BODY

■ **Unscramble each word. Use the clues in parentheses to help you. Then, use the boxed letters to find the secret word that means "a person who walks."**

1. pntlasnart (transfer) __ __ __ __ __ ☐ __ __ __ __

2. cermemond (suggest) __ ☐ __ __ __ __ __ __ __

3. deresint (occupant) __ __ __ ☐ __ __ __ __

4. duardqpue (anything with four legs) __ __ __ __ __ __ ☐ __ __

5. erattsu (height) ☐ __ __ __ __ __ __

6. ssoudntarlu (high-pitched frequencies) __ __ ☐ __ __ __ __ __ __ __ __

7. dotarrhpo (insect or spider) __ ☐ __ __ __ __ __ __

8. manista (strength) __ __ __ __ ☐ __ __

9. zadmae (surprised) __ __ ☐ __ __ __

10. muosrnoe (gigantic) __ ☐ __ __ __ __ __

Name_____ Date_____

REVIEW: ENGINEERING, SCIENCE & THE BODY

■ **Use the clues to complete the puzzle.**

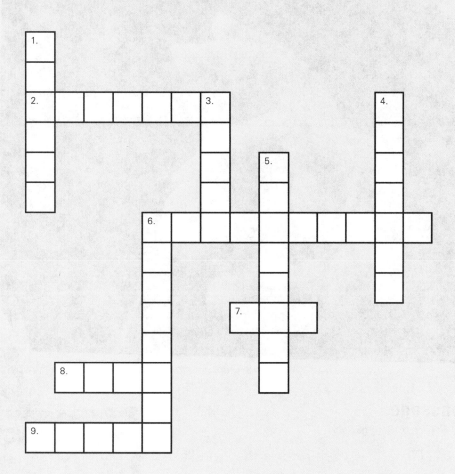

ACROSS

2. Adjective meaning "twisted," like tree roots
6. These flowers made a statement.
7. Acronym for a place that has its own weather
8. Means "dreams"
9. You breathe in oxygen with these.

DOWN

1. Not a real dog
3. Someone who gives
4. City to visit the whale sharks
5. Average woman here is 5 feet 2 inches (157 cm)
6. Relatives of Arachnoscelis

FANCY FUNGI

■ Read the passage.

Most Expensive Fungus Species

The white truffle (*Tuber magnum pico*) is the world's Most Expensive **Fungus** Species. This fancy fungus sells for up to $1,500 a pound (454 g). It is found almost exclusively in the Piedmont region of Italy.

Truffles are like mushrooms. But, instead of growing aboveground, they grow beneath it. They are found about 12 inches (30 cm) underground and grow in the roots of trees.

The white truffle is called the "diamond of the table." White truffles have a strong aroma and an intense flavor. They are never cooked and always served raw. Most white truffles are about the size of walnuts, but some can be as big as oranges. These truffles are the most expensive because they are rare and delicate. They are very **perishable** and taste best when eaten within three days of being found.

DID YOU KNOW?

Truffle hunters use dogs to help them find truffles. The dogs are trained to sniff out the truffles. Once the dog has discovered one, she will use her paws to start digging. The hunter then takes over and uses a shovel to dig. He doesn't want the dog damaging the precious truffle or gobbling it up like a doggie treat!

Name_____ Date_____

■ **Answer the questions.**

1. What is a truffle?_____

2. How are truffles like mushrooms? How are they different?_____

_____

3. A **fungus** can be a:
   A. mushroom
   B. mold
   C. truffle
   D. all of the above

4. Circle *F* for fact or *O* for opinion.

   A. Truffles have a great flavor.   F   O

   B. The white truffle is called the "diamond of the table."   F   O

   C. Truffle hunters love animals.   F   O

5. Circle *T* for true or *F* for false.

   A. Truffles are found underground.   T   F

   B. White truffles are found just about everywhere trees are.   T   F

   C. White truffles are eaten raw.   T   F

6. The passage states that truffles are **perishable**. What other types of foods are perishable?

_____

_____

■ **Choose one extension activity.**
   A. Dogs work to help truffle hunters find truffles. Find articles about dogs that have other jobs.
   B. Imagine that you own a company that sells white truffles. Write a commercial or design an advertisement about them.

THE HUMAN LIGHTNING ROD

■ Read the passage.
Most Lightning Strikes Survived, June 25, 1977

Whoever said that lightning doesn't strike in the same place twice? It certainly wasn't Roy C. Sullivan! Sullivan (USA) holds the Guinness World Records™ record for Most Lightning Strikes Survived. He was struck by lightning seven times between 1942 and 1983. Sullivan worked as a park ranger in Shenandoah National Park, Virginia.

Lightning happens when a giant amount of electricity is released, and usually occurs during a thunderstorm. A single lightning strike is made of several hundred million volts. A **volt** is the unit that measures voltage, or electrical energy.

The chance of being struck by lightning is 1 in 700,000. Each year about 100 people lose their lives to lightning in the United States alone. Most of these deaths are in Florida, the lightning capital of the United States

The best place to be during a lightning storm is indoors. If you are outdoors and hear thunder, get inside a building or vehicle. If you cannot, then stay away from water and metal objects. Get to a low area or crouch down near a group of short trees.

DID YOU KNOW?
Before people knew what thunder and lightning were, there were some interesting myths. The ancient Greeks thought the god Zeus threw lightning bolts. Vikings believed that the god Thor hit his giant hammer while he rode across the sky. Some American Indians thought that a mystical bird's flashing feathers caused lightning.

Name_____ Date_____

■ Answer the questions.

1. When does lightning happen?_____

_____

2. What state in the United States has the most accidents due

to lightning?_____

_____

3. A **volt** is:
   A. lightning
   B. an animal
   C. a unit of electricity
   D. a city in Greece

4. Circle *T* for true or *F* for false.

   A. A lightning strike is made of one hundred
      million volts.   T   F

   B. The ancient Greeks thought Zeus caused lightning.   T   F

   C. Roy C. Sullivan was struck by lightning seven times.   T   F

5. Where did Roy C. Sullivan work? How do you think that Sullivan's job could have played a part
   in his world record?

   _____

   _____

6. Where is the best place to be during a lightning storm? What should you stay away from?

   _____

   _____

■ Choose one extension activity.

A. Interesting myths were created before people knew what lightning really was. Use
   your imagination to write your own creative explanation of what could cause lightning.

B. Design a safety poster to help children avoid the dangers of lightning.

A-MAZE-ING

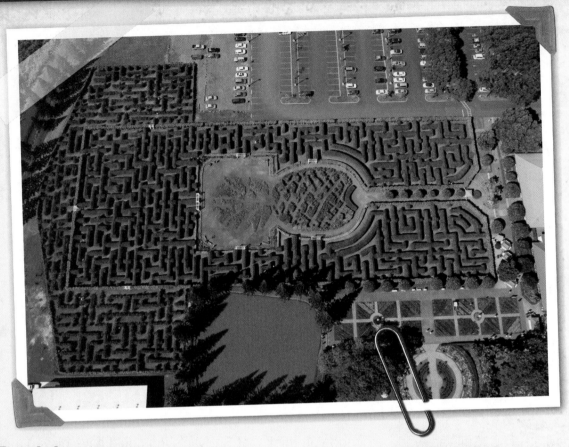

■ Read the passage.
Largest Maze, Permanent Hedge Maze, July 2007

If you're looking for a challenge, head to Hawaii. The world's largest permanent hedge maze is in Wahiawa, Oahu. The Pineapple Garden Maze is on the **plantation** of a major fruit company.

A maze is a puzzle. When players enter a maze, they try to follow the path to the end. It is not easy getting to the end of a good maze. Mazes contain twists and turns to confuse the players. It is easy to get lost!

The Pineapple Garden Maze includes 14,000 Hawaiian plants. When it opened in 1997, it was 1.7 miles (2.8 km) long. The fruit company expanded it in 2007. The maze is now 3.15 acres, and its path is a total length of about 2.5 miles (3.9 km). The maze walls are over 6 feet (2 m) high.

The Pineapple Garden Maze is more than just a maze. In addition to getting to the end of the maze, players try to find hidden clue stations. The clues help them solve the mystery of the maze.

DID YOU KNOW?
A maze can be formed from different things. The walls can be plants, stones, or even snow. A maze also can be printed on paper. A player uses a finger, a pen, or a pencil to make a path through it.

Name_____ Date_____

■ **Answer the questions.**

1. What is the Pineapple Garden maze made of? _____

_____

2. Where is the Pineapple Garden maze?_____

_____

3. Another word for **plantation** is:

   A. market
   B. farm
   C. kitchen
   D. house

4. Circle *T* for true or *F* for false.

   A. The Pineapple Garden Maze is a hedge maze.   T   F

   B. All mazes are easy.   T   F

   C. The Pineapple Garden Maze is made of 140 plants.   T   F

5. What is the point of trying to get through a maze? Have you ever tried to get to the end of a maze? What skills did you use to help you?

_____

_____

_____

6. Mazes can be made from many different types of material. What qualities would make a material good for maze building? Why?

_____

_____

■ **Choose one extension activity.**

A. The Pineapple Garden Maze is a permanent maze. Research other permanent mazes around the world. Where are they? What are they made of? How do they compare with the Pineapple Garden Maze?

B. Design and draw your own maze.

© Carson-Dellosa

RIDING HIGH

■ Read the passage.
Driving to the Highest Altitude by Car, April 21, 2007

Imagine being four miles (6.4 km) in the air without a plane. Before you panic, you should know that these record-breakers were driving a car. Gonzalo Bravo (Chile) and Eduardo Canales (Chile) hold the Guinness World Records™ record for driving to the highest **altitude** by car. Their 1986 Suzuki Samurai made it up 21,942 feet (6,688 m). Bravo drove the car. Eduardo was the "co-driver." They broke the record driving up a volcano in Chile. The volcano is called the Ojos del Salado. Ojos del Salado means *eyes of the salty mountain*.

Bravo and Canales prepared for almost a year before taking the trip. Bravo worked very hard on the car. He added special parts to give the car more power.

The journey was not easy. The **terrain** of the volcano was very rough. The car had to make it over huge rocks, sand, snow, and glaciers.

DID YOU KNOW?
Going up high can cause people to become sick. The higher a person goes, the thinner the air. Thinner air means less oxygen. Breathing is difficult with less oxygen in the air. The best way to climb is to go up gradually. A person's body can adjust to higher altitudes if going up is a slow process.

Name_____ Date_____

■ Answer the questions.

1. What did Bravo do to prepare for the trip? _____

_____

2. What made the journey up the volcano difficult? _____

_____

3. Altitude means:

   A. elevation

   B. width

   C. shape

   D. size

4. The volcano's **terrain** is its:

   A. lava

   B. surface

   C. power

   D. smoke

5. How can being up high cause a person to get sick? Have you felt sick when you were up high? Explain your experience.

_____

_____

_____

6. What is the volcano's name? What does it mean in English? Why do you think it might have been given that name?

_____

_____

7. Which member of the team was the "co-driver"? What do you think that a "co-driver" does?

_____

_____

■ Choose one extension activity.

  A. Research changes that can be made to a go-kart to give it "special power" for climbing.

  B. Imagine that you are driving this car up the volcano. Describe your experiences as you climb to the top.

HURRICANE KATRINA

■ Read the passage.
Worst Cyclone Disaster—Damage Toll, August 29, 2005

Hurricane Katrina hit the southeastern United States on August 29, 2005. Katrina holds the Guinness World Records™ record for the Worst Cyclone Disaster based on the amount of damage. The damage from the hurricane was **astronomical**. It cost an estimated 81 billion dollars.

Katrina was the third deadliest natural disaster in U.S. history. Power lines were down. Cities were flooded. Homes and buildings were destroyed. About 1,800 people lost their lives. Most of these were in Louisiana. New Orleans, Louisiana, was hit the worst.

Katrina was a monster storm. It quickly went from Category 1 to Category 5. Category 5 is the highest possible rating. Winds blew at 140 miles (225 km) per hour. Katrina created 43 tornadoes. More than one million people had to **evacuate** their homes because of the storm.

DID YOU KNOW?

Cyclones have different names around the world. In the Western Pacific, they are called typhoons. In the Atlantic and Eastern Pacific, they are called hurricanes. The eye is the center of a hurricane. Winds rotate around the eye. They move in a counter-clockwise direction. If winds reach 40 miles (64 km) per hour, it is a tropical storm. Once they hit 74 miles (119 km) per hour, it is a hurricane.

Name_____ Date_____

■ Answer the questions.

1. Where did Hurricane Katrina strike? _____

_____

2. How fast were the winds from Katrina? How fast must winds be to classify a storm as a hurricane?

_____

3. **Evacuate** means to:
   A. leave one's home
   B. go on vacation
   C. be in a vacuum
   D. be vaccinated

4. Another word for **astronomical** is:
   A. enormous
   B. little
   C. normal
   D. shiny

5. Circle *T* for true or *F* for false.

   A. Hurricane Katrina was the third deadliest disaster to hit the U.S.   T   F

   B. Many people in Louisiana lost their lives to the hurricane.   T   F

   C. Hurricane Katrina cost less money than any other hurricane in U.S. history.   T   F

6. Katrina quickly went from a Category 1 rating to a Category 5. What does that mean?

_____

_____

■ Choose one extension activity.

A. Use a map to trace Hurricane Katrina's path. Mark where the hurricane was its strongest and where the most damage occurred.

B. Research hurricanes to learn what causes them.

A GARDEN FOR A GIANT

■ Read the passage.

Heaviest Squash, September 21, 2007
Heaviest Celery, August 27, 2003
Heaviest Kale, August 29, 2007

Imagine a vegetable garden with veggies fit for a giant. These Guinness World Records™ record-breaking vegetables are something right out of a storybook.

Bradley Wursten (Netherlands) grew a squash to squash all others. The squash weighed 1,234 pounds (560 kg). It holds the Guinness World Record for Heaviest Squash. He grew the **massive** vegetable in 2007.

The world's Heaviest Celery weighed 63 pounds 5 ounces (28.7 kg). Scott and Mardie Robb (USA) grew the celery. They presented it at the Alaska State Fair in 2003.

At the 2007 Alaska State Fair, Scott Robb won the prize for the world's Heaviest Kale. Kale is a leafy green vegetable similar to lettuce or spinach. Robb's kale weighed 105 pounds (48 kg).

DID YOU KNOW?
Giant vegetables are not for eating. Their flavors are not as rich as smaller vegetables. They usually taste bitter. **Colossal** vegetables are grown for fun and for competition.

© Carson-Dellosa

Name_____ Date_____

■ Answer the questions.

1. What vegetables are mentioned in the passage? _____
   _____

2. Do people normally eat giant vegetables? Why or why not?_____
   _____

3. **Colossal** is to **massive** as tiny is to:
   - **A.** huge
   - **B.** miniature
   - **C.** gigantic
   - **D.** enormous

4. Circle *F* for fact or *O* for opinion.

   A. Giant squash is delicious.   F   O

   B. Europeans love giant vegetables.   F   O

   C. The heaviest squash was grown in 2007.   F   O

5. If giant vegetables are not for eating, what could be some alternative uses for these record-breakers?
   _____
   _____
   _____

6. Do you think that important information is missing from the passage? What other facts would you like to know about these records?
   _____
   _____
   _____

■ Choose one extension activity.

A. The author asks you to imagine a vegetable garden fit for a giant. Draw this imaginary vegetable garden.

B. What giant vegetable would be fun to grow? Write about some of the challenges you might face.

THE LONGEST DAY

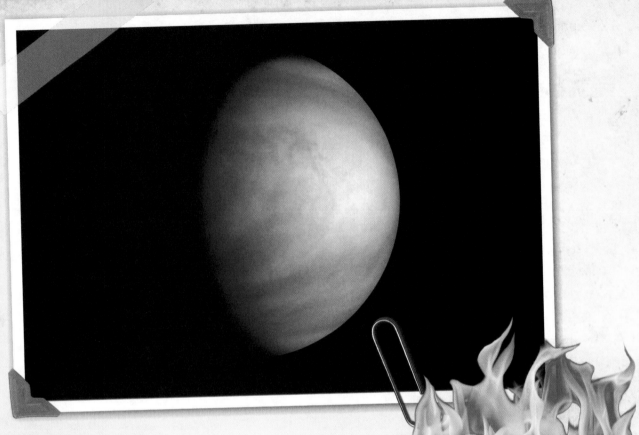

■ **Read the passage.**
Planet with the Longest Day

Have you ever had a long day? If you lived on Venus, every day would feel long. Venus holds the Guinness World Records™ record for the planet with the longest day. One day on Venus is the same as 243 days on Earth!

A day is measured by how long a planet takes to completely rotate on its axis. Earth takes 23 hours and 56 minutes to complete one rotation. But, Venus takes 243 "Earth days" to do the same thing. Venus spins at a snail's pace.

A year is the time it takes a planet to orbit the sun. A day on Venus is longer than its year. That means that it takes Venus longer to spin around once than to travel all the way around the sun. Since it is closer to the sun, the length of a year on Venus is shorter than a year on Earth. A year on Venus lasts 224.7 Earth days. That means it takes 224.7 Earth days for Venus to orbit the sun once.

DID YOU KNOW?
Venus, the second planet from the sun, is the hottest planet in our solar system. The temperature on Venus gets up to an **astounding** 896°F (480°C).

© Carson-Dellosa

Name_____ Date_____

■ Answer the questions.

1. How many Earth days equal one year on Venus? _____

_____

2. How is a day measured?_____

_____

3. A synonym for the word **astounding** is:
   A. amazing
   B. regular
   C. normal
   D. average

4. Circle *T* for true or *F* for false.

   A. Venus spins quickly.   **T**   **F**

   B. The temperature on Venus is very comfortable.   **T**   **F**

   C. A day on Venus is longer than one Earth year.   **T**   **F**

5. In your opinion, how would life on Venus be different from life on Earth?

_____

_____

_____

6. Do you think that it is important to learn about planets? Why or why not?

_____

_____

_____

■ Choose one extension activity.

A. Research other planets in our solar system. How do their days and years compare to those of Earth and Venus?

B. Create a K-W-L chart for Venus. List what you already knew (K) in the first column, what you want to know (W) in the second column, and what you learned (L) from reading the passage in the third column.

Name_____ Date_____

REVIEW: EARTH EXTREMES

■ **Find the words hidden in the puzzle. The words may be found across, down, and diagonally.**

altitude	colossal	perishable
astounding	evacuate	plantation
astronomical	fungus	Venus
terrain	lightning	volt

```
a d g o m n x o p c u s p m
t s p l a n t a t i o n e j
e g t m a p q v e n u s v r
r x n r m l k r t h r k a l
r g w m o y t m i n b b c i
a s t o u n d i n g y d u g
i v m f x q o w t k b j a h
n z o t u s h m t u d i t t
j u b w n n c o i w d y e n
g p l g x k g w f c m e p i
z v q v o l t u g m a h u n
r m n h c o l o s s a l t g
y r l m t o c e u g r d r o
e p e r i s h a b l e l w i
```

74

© Carson-Dellosa

REVIEW: EARTH EXTREMES

■ **Use the clues to complete the puzzle.**

ACROSS

2. Ojos del Salado is one.
4. Vikings believed he caused thunder and lightning.
7. Giant vegetable fair state
8. Katrina hit this state hardest.
9. Center of a hurricane

DOWN

1. Diamond of the table
2. This planet is a scorcher.
3. Truffle hunter's best friend
6. You might get lost in the hedges in this state.

SKILLED SKATER

■ Read the passage.

Most Consecutive Skateboard Front-side Ollies (Half-pipe), September 20, 2008

Keith Baldassare (USA) wanted to break a skateboard record. He did more than break it. He crushed it! The record was for Most Consecutive Skateboard Front-side Ollies on a Half-Pipe. The previous record was 46. Baldassare did 348! He was 13 years old when he broke the Guinness World Records™ record.

Baldassare started skateboarding when he was seven years old. His neighbor was skateboarding, and Baldassare looked up to him. So, he started to practice. Baldassare got the idea to break the record after seeing the previous record-holder on TV.

Baldassare combined his record-breaking event with fund-raising. The event raised money for Grind for Life, an organization that helps cancer patients and their families. When patients have to travel for treatment, Grind for Life helps pay the travel expenses.

Baldassare had **aspired** to beat the record, and that's just what he did! But, at the same time, Baldassare raised money for a good cause.

DID YOU KNOW?

Front-side is a skateboard move that keeps the body facing the ramp or the obstacle while doing a trick. An *ollie* is a jump performed by tapping the tail of the board on the ground. A *half-pipe* is a U-shaped ramp that usually has a flat section in the middle.

Name_____ Date_____

■ Answer the questions.

1. What is Grind for Life?_____
_____

2. Who inspired Keith Baldassare to start skateboarding?_____
_____

3. Describe a front-side ollie on a half-pipe._____
_____
_____

4. Aspired means:

    A. walked gently

    B. tried to achieve a goal

    C. gave up

    D. felt jealous

5. Circle *T* for true or *F* for false.

    A. Baldassare raised money for a cause while breaking the record.   **T**   **F**

    B. A half-pipe is a term for a skateboarder who is also a plumber.   **T**   **F**

    C. Baldassare started skateboarding at age 10.   **T**   **F**

6. Did you ever start doing something because of someone you admired? What was it? Do you still enjoy doing it?

_____
_____
_____

■ Choose one extension activity.

A. Research other skateboarding tricks and records.

B. If you could interview Baldassare, what questions would you ask? What do you think his answers might be?

SPIN MASTER

■ Read the passage.

Most Basketballs Spun Simultaneously on a Frame, May 25, 1999

Michael Kettman (USA) has his hands full! He holds the Guinness World Records™ record for Most Basketballs Spun **Simultaneously** on a Frame. He spun 28 basketballs in 1999. Kettman kept all 28 balls spinning for five seconds.

Kettman was born in Illinois. When he was four years old, he saw the Harlem Globetrotters perform. One of the team's star players, Curley Neal, became his hero. Kettman was inspired and taught himself to spin.

When Kettman was 15 years old, the record for spinning the most basketballs was eight. Kettman decided that he wanted to break it. He started practicing six to eight hours a day. Soon, he could spin 10 balls and became the new Guinness World Record holder. Kettman's record was broken a few years later. But, he refused to give up, so he started spinning again. In 1997, he spun 20 balls, then 25. Finally, in 1999, he spun 28 balls.

Previous Guinness World Record holders had spun balls on nails attached to body pads. But, Kettman thought differently about spinning to break the record. He built a special frame with plastic pipes. The balls spin on top of nails in the frame. The whole frame sits on his lap. Kettman's new design helped him earn this Guinness World Record.

Name_____ Date_____

■ **Answer the questions.**

1. What was the first record that Michael Kettman broke?_____
_____

2. What is the greatest number of balls that Kettman has spun simultaneously? _____
_____

3. **Simultaneously** means:
   A. at the same time
   B. too many
   C. for a long time
   D. quickly

4. Circle *T* for true or *F* for false.

   A. A Harlem Globetrotter inspired Kettman to spin basketballs.   T   F

   B. Kettman broke his first record when he was 13 years old.   T   F

   C. Kettman practiced at least six hours a day.   T   F

5. What is different about the way Kettman spins balls compared to previous record-holders?

   _____

   _____

6. What skills do you think that Kettman has to help him spin so many balls? Have you tried to spin a ball on your finger? What made it difficult?

   _____

   _____

■ **Choose one extension activity.**

A. Try spinning a ball on your finger. Time how long you can spin it.

B. Design a different device that might help a person spin a lot of basketballs at once. Draw your design in action.

TRICKS UP THEIR SLEEVES

■ Read the passage.

Youngest Person to Win the Wild West Arts' Texas Skip Race, 2006

Largest Trick Roping Loop by a Female, 2003

Cody Lamb (USA) was an 11-year-old cowboy from Jerome, Idaho, when he broke the Guinness World Records™ record for Youngest Person to Win the Wild West Arts' Texas Skip Race. The skip race takes place at the Will Rogers Wild West International Expo in Oklahoma.

Texas skip racing is a type of trick roping. Trick roping has been around for a long time. It is done for fun, entertainment, and competition. To do the Texas Skip, performers spin a lasso and make a wide loop. They move the loop from side to side and skip through it as they race.

Lamb is not the only one in his family with an **aptitude** for performing. Lamb's mother, Kimberly Mink (USA), holds a world record. She broke the Guinness World Record for Largest Trick Roping Loop by a Female. Kimberly spun a loop around her, fed to a length of 76 feet (23 m).

DID YOU KNOW?
Trick roping was losing popularity at the beginning of the twentieth century. Now, thanks to the Wild West Arts Club, trick roping is becoming popular again.

Name_____ Date_____

■ Answer the questions.

1. What record did Cody Lamb break? _____

_____

2. Who else in Lamb's family holds a world record?_____

_____

3. **Aptitude** means:

    A. dislike

    B. luck

    C. dull

    D. skill

4. Circle *T* for true or *F* for false.

    A. Cody Lamb's family has talented performers.   T   F

    B. Texas Skip involves spinning a lasso.   T   F

    C. Lamb's mother has an award for trick rope jumping.   T   F

5. Lamb's family is a family of performers. Imagine that you and your family are performers. What might your family win awards for?

_____

_____

■ Choose one extension activity.

A. Texas Skip is a type of trick roping. Research other types of trick roping.

B. See if you can make a loop big enough to try the Texas Skip. Can you do any other tricks with rope?

GO, GO, GO-KART

■ Read the passage.
Karting—Greatest Distance in 24 Hours (Outdoor), September 21, 2007

Go-karts are small, open, four-wheel motorized vehicles used for racing. A team of four drivers who call themselves Equipe Vitesse holds the Guinness World Records™ record for the farthest distance by kart in 24 hours outdoors. The team drove 1,277.97 miles (2,056.7 km) on a track in the United Kingdom.

Russell Crowe, Joe Flay, Simon Rudd, and Tom Huxtable are the drivers. They have won many races together. They have won the **prestigious** Le Mans 24-hour race four times in the last six years.

Equipe Vitesse broke the record in a kart that had a five-speed Honda CR125 engine. The drivers chose an engine that was great for speed but not so reliable for distance. They planned to replace the engine throughout the race whenever it broke down. They thought that this was the best choice. Obviously, they made the right decision. Throughout the course of the race, the team had to change the engine three times. But, that didn't stop them from breaking the record.

DID YOU KNOW?
Karting has been around since the 1950s. The first go-kart manufacturer opened in 1958. The first go-kart engine was made from a chain saw. In the 1960s, motorcycle engines were used for karts. Later, companies started making engines especially for go-karts.

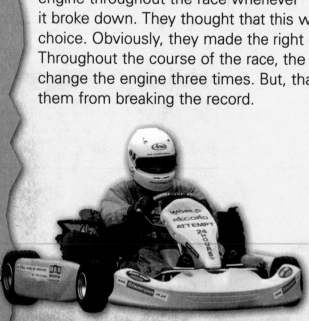

Name_____ Date_____

■ **Answer the questions.**

1. Who is Equipe Vitesse?_____
_____

2. Write three adjectives to describe a go-kart. _____
_____

3. Another word for **prestigious** is:
   A. horrible
   B. respected
   C. dangerous
   D. organized

4. Circle *T* for true or *F* for false.

   A. Go-karts were invented in the 1960s.   T   F

   B. The first go-kart engine was made from a chain saw.   T   F

   C. Go-karts are normally very large vehicles.   T   F

5. What characteristics of the engine did the drivers decide they wanted for the record-breaking race? What did they consider when making this decision?
_____
_____

6. The team had to make a choice about the engine that they used. What other decisions do you think that they had to make before racing?
_____
_____

7. How many members make up team Equipe Vitesse? Why do you think they need this number of people?
_____
_____

■ **Choose one statement. Then, explain why you agree or disagree.**

   A. All eight-year-olds should be allowed to participate in go-kart racing.
   B. A special driving test should be given to anyone who wants to race go-karts.

83

CARTWHEELING TEEN

■ Read the passage.
Most Cartwheels in One Hour, August 13, 2007

If people spin cartwheels when they are happy, Ivan Koveshnikov (USA) must be overjoyed. Ivan holds the Guinness World Records™ record for doing the most cartwheels in one hour. He completed 1,714 of them.

Ivan Koveshnikov was born in Moscow, Russia, and moved to the United States in 1992. When he **achieved** the world record in 2007, he was 18 years old.

Koveshnikov has always loved setting challenges for himself. Before breaking the Guinness World Record, he wrote a list of goals. The list contained items such as: rip a telephone book in half, visit every continent, and break a world record. Koveshnikov decided to focus on breaking a world record.

The previous Guinness World Record for Most Cartwheels in One Hour was 1,297. Koveshnikov put a lot of work into breaking it. He didn't want to beat the record by only a few cartwheels. He wanted to win by a **landslide**. He knew that he had to complete about 22 cartwheels per minute. He ended up doing more than 28 per minute. To prevent dizziness, Koveshnikov switched direction every 50 cartwheels.

Name_____ Date_____

■ Answer the questions.

1. How did Ivan Koveshnikov prevent dizziness? _____
_____

2. How many cartwheels did Koveshnikov do per minute?_____
_____

3. If you "win by a **landslide**" you
    A. win by a little.
    B. tie for first place.
    C. win by sliding.
    D. win by a lot.

4. An antonym for **achieved** is:
    A. succeeded
    B. gained
    C. overcame
    D. failed

5. Circle *F* for fact or *O* for opinion.

    A. Cartwheels are fun.   **F**   **O**

    B. Koveshnikov was smart to figure out how many cartwheels
        he would have to do in a minute.   **F**   **O**

    C. Koveshnikov wrote a list of goals for himself.   **F**   **O**

6. Koveshnikov loves setting challenges for himself. Describe a challenge that you set for
yourself. Did you achieve it?

_____

_____

_____

■ Choose one extension activity.
A. Write a list of five goals for yourself. What goal on the
list would you attempt first?
B. Try to do a cartwheel. Partner with a friend to see how
many you can do in a minute.

BOLD BREAK DANCING

■ Read the passage.
Most Elbow Spins, August 19, 2005

Mark Dossenbach (Switzerland) rolls up his sleeves and puts his elbows to work. Dossenbach is a break-dancer who holds the Guinness World Records™ record for Most Elbow Spins. In 2005, he performed 16 **continuous** spins on his elbows in Zug, Switzerland.

A spin is a break-dance move where dancers rotate their bodies in the air while staying in contact with the ground. A dancer can perform a spin with any part of the body touching the floor. However, performing on exposed skin can slow down the spin and can hurt. Many break-dancers use pieces of cloth or pads to prevent this.

After a wrist injury, Dossenbach started spinning on his elbows instead of using his hands. He wears pads on his elbows. Dossenbach trained to break the record by practicing for at least one hour a day for eight years.

DID YOU KNOW?
Break dancing is an inventive style of dance. Dancers use their imaginations to come up with new moves and to make their routines unique.

■ Answer the questions.

1. What is a spin?_____

_____

_____

2. What problems can dancers have if they spin on exposed skin? _____

_____

3. An antonym for the word **continuous** is:

   A. nonstop

   B. interrupted

   C. few

   D. many

4. Circle *T* for true or *F* for false.

   A. Mark Dossenbach performed 16 continuous spins on his elbows.   **T**   **F**

   B. Dossenbach wears pads on his hands.   **T**   **F**

   C. A spin can be done with any part of the body touching the floor.   **T**   **F**

5. Have you ever seen someone break-dance? Compare and contrast break dancing to other styles of dancing.

_____

_____

6. How can you fix a slow spin?

_____

_____

■ Choose one extension activity.

A. Create a unique dance move of your own. Invent a name for your new move.

B. Research the names and descriptions of other break-dance moves.

STRETCHED OUT SNOWBOARD

■ Read the passage.
Largest Snowboard, March 18, 2007

Would you like to have a party with friends while snowboarding? This snowboard is big enough to do just that! Arnold Schindler and his team hold the Guinness World Records™ record for the Largest Snowboard. Their board measures 33 feet (10 m) long and 7 feet (2.15 m) wide. Most snowboards are about 5 feet (1.5 m) long.

How was the first snowboard developed? The **origin** of the snowboard is not simple. In 1964, a surfer named Sherman Poppen imagined surfing on the Rocky Mountains of North America. The idea inspired Poppen, so he built a surfboard for the snow. The "Snurfer" was created from two kids' skis bolted together. It was about 4 feet (1.2 m) long and made of plastic. One million Snurfers were sold in the following 10 years. But, soon the product disappeared.

In 1970, Dimitrije Milovich was having fun in New York sliding on the snow on a cafeteria tray. This gave him an idea. He made a short surfboard for the snow. He formed the first snowboard company. Snowboards manufactured by different companies continued to develop over the years into the boards that we know today.

> **DID YOU KNOW?**
> The first official snowboarding competition was held in Colorado in 1981. Snowboarding became a winter sport in the 1998 Olympic Games.

Name_____ Date_____

■ Answer the questions.

1. How big is the world's Largest Snowboard? _____

_____

2. Who invented the first version of a snowboard? _____

_____

3. **Origin** means:
   A. source
   B. owner
   C. winter
   D. fact

4. Circle *T* for true or *F* for false.

   A. The first snowboard was called a *Snurfer*.   T   F

   B. Dimitrije Milovich started the first snowboard company.   T   F

   C. Snowboarding was popular before surfboarding.   T   F

5. Think of other names that the original snowboard could have been named.

_____

_____

6. The inventor of the first snowboard imagined surfing over the Rockies. He loved to surf and wanted to combine this with riding down a mountain. What are your two favorite things to do? Try combining them to describe an idea for a new sport or hobby.

_____

_____

■ Choose one extension activity.

A. Snowboarding became an Olympic sport in 1998. Research snowboarding's growth in the Olympics. What are the most recent snowboarding events? How has snowboarding changed over the years?

B. Do you think someone could ride the Largest Snowboard down a mountain? Would this be safe? Why or why not?

RIVER SWIMMER

■ **Read the passage.**
**Longest Journey Swimming,
April 8, 2007**

Imagine swimming every day for two months. For Martin Strel (Slovenia), it is no sweat. He holds the Guinness World Records™ record for Longest Journey Swimming. He swam the entire length of the Amazon River! The distance covered was 3,273 miles (5,268 km). That is longer than the width of the Atlantic Ocean. The 2007 journey took him about two months. He started on February 1 and finished on April 8.

Strel is a long-distance swimmer and has swum the lengths of many rivers. He sleeps for only five hours a day when taking on a river like the Amazon.

Strel likes talking to people about the Amazon River. He wants to **persuade** people to stop the destruction of the environment. He has been raising money for this cause. His **motto** is, "Swimming for peace, friendship, and clean waters."

DID YOU KNOW?
The Amazon River is in South America. It is one of the two longest rivers on Earth. The other longest river is the Nile in Africa. The Amazon carries more water than any other river and is also known as the River Sea.

Name_____ Date_____

■ Answer the questions.

1. How long did it take Martin Strel to swim the Amazon River? _____

_____

2. Why does Strel like talking to people about his experience on the river? _____

_____

3. Another word for **persuade** is:

    A. influence

    B. talk

    C. scare

    D. ask

4. Circle *T* for true or *F* for false.

    A. The Amazon is the world's largest sea.   **T**   **F**

    B. Strel has swum the lengths of many rivers.   **T**   **F**

    C. Strel holds the Guinness World Record for
        swimming across the Atlantic Ocean.   **T**   **F**

5. What do you think Strel had to do to prepare for a journey like this one? What are some of the obstacles he might have faced?

_____

_____

_____

6. Do you think Strel's plan to swim the Amazon River is a good way to raise money and awareness for his cause? Why or why not? What are other ways that he could achieve this?

_____

_____

■ Choose one extension activity.

A. A **motto** is a personal statement that explains what a person believes in. Strel's motto is "Swimming for peace, friendship, and clean waters." Do you have a motto? Think about something you strongly believe in and write your own motto.

B. Research the Amazon River and find out what kinds of animals and plants Strel might have seen while swimming the river.

RIDE THE WHEEL

■ Read the passage.
Fastest Monowheel Motorcycle

The monowheel only looks like it is made for a giant hamster. But, it can actually be driven—and fast! Just ask Kerry McLean (USA). McLean holds the Guinness World Records™ record for highest speed reached on a monowheel motorcycle. McLean drove his monowheel 57 miles (92 km) per hour. McLean set this record at Irwindale Speedway in California.

A monowheel is one large wheel. *Mono-* is a prefix meaning "one." The word *monowheel* **literally** means "one wheel." A monowheel is similar to a unicycle. But, instead of sitting above the wheel, a monowheel rider sits inside or next to it. The wheel revolves around a track. That momentum is how a monowheel moves. A monowheel motorcycle is a monowheel powered by an engine. The engine sits inside the wheel along with the rider.

The monowheel that McLean rode to set the record was 48 inches (1.22 m) in diameter. An old snowmobile engine powered the bike.

> ## DID YOU KNOW?
> Today, monowheels are built for fun and for entertainment. But, from the 1860s to the 1930s, they were used as a real **mode** of transportation.

Name_____ Date_____

Answer the questions.

1. Where did Kerry McLean set the Guinness World Record for highest speed by a monowheel motorcycle? _____

2. Where does a monowheel rider sit? _____

_____

3. A **mode** is:
   - A. a method
   - B. a car
   - C. a motorcycle
   - D. a game

4. **Literally** means:
   - A. symbolic
   - B. word for word
   - C. difficult
   - D. confusing

5. Circle *F* for fact or *O* for opinion.

   A. Monowheels are amazing.   F   O

   B. Monowheels have been around since the 1800s.   F   O

   C. A monowheel motorcycle is powered by an engine.   F   O

6. What does the prefix *mono-* mean? Use the dictionary to list other words beginning with *mono-*.

_____

_____

7. What safety measures would you suggest to a driver trying to get a monowheel motorcycle up to a high speed? _____

_____

Choose one extension activity.
A. Research monowheels throughout history.
B. Write a newspaper advertisement of 25 words or less describing a used monowheel for sale.

Name _____ Date _____

REVIEW: GAME TIME!

■ **Use the code and the context clues to complete the missing vocabulary words. Some of the letters are already filled in.**

Symbol	▲	⬡	●	■	♦	▬	✕	←	★	∧	✓	✳	❖	✛	>	<
Letter					S	I	E				D		N	O		

1. I __ __ __ __ __ __ to be a famous writer.
▲ ♦ ⬡ ✕ ● ←

2. Can you walk and juggle __ __ __ __ __ __ __ __ __ __ __ __ __ __ ?
♦ ✕ ■ ▬ ★ ∧ ▲ ✛ ← > ■ ♦ ★ ✓

3. She has an __ __ __ __ __ __ __ __ for cooking.
▲ ⬡ ∧ ✕ ∧ ▬ ✳ ←

4. That is a __ __ __ __ __ __ __ __ __ __ __ __ award.
⬡ ● ← ♦ ✕ ∧ ✕ ❖ ✕ > ▬ ♦

5. Our team won by a __ __ __ __ __ __ __ __ __ .
★ ▲ ✛ ✳ ♦ ★ ✕ ✳ ←

6. When I said I had a splitting headache, I didn't mean it in a
__ __ __ __ __ __ __ way.
★ ✕ ∧ ← ● ▲ ★

7. Do you know the __ __ __ __ __ __ of that folktale?
> ● ✕ ❖ ✕ ✛

8. I was able to __ __ __ __ __ __ __ __ my parents to let me go.
⬡ ← ● ♦ ▬ ▲ ✳ ←

9. The __ __ __ __ __ __ __ __ __ __ barking kept us awake all night.
< > ✛ ∧ ✕ ✛ ▬ > ▬ ♦

Name_____ Date_____

REVIEW: GAME TIME!

■ **Use the clues to complete the puzzle.**

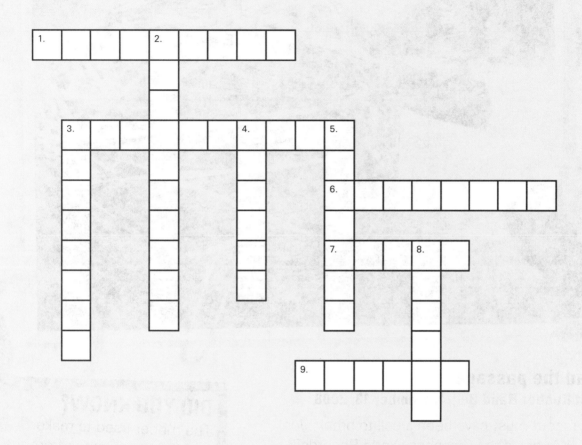

ACROSS

1. _____ racing is a type of trick roping.
3. The record number of these done in one hour is 1,774.
6. A monowheel is similar to one.
7. It sits on Kettman's lap.
9. Martin Strel's river

DOWN

2. What Keith Baldassare rides
3. First go-kart engine
4. Mark Dossenbach spins on them.
5. First snowboard?
8. Cartwheel spinner was born here.

HAVING A BALL

■ Read the passage.
Largest Rubber Band Ball, November 13, 2008

This record must have been a ball to break. Joel Waul (USA) holds the Guinness World Records™ record for the Largest Rubber Band Ball. The ball is over 6 feet (2 m) tall and weighs 9,032 pounds (4,097 kg). It is made of just rubber bands—over 700,000 of them! The rubber bands Waul used came in various sizes and colors.

Waul was working at a clothing store when he got the idea to make the ball. He saw on television a giant rubber band ball dropped from an airplane. He spent almost six years working on his ball. He wrapped and stretched each rubber band around and around until he had formed the giant ball. He built it in the driveway of his home in Florida.

Waul sold his ball to a museum. The museum had to use a crane and a flatbed truck to move it. Waul is happy about the idea that people from all over will be able to enjoy his **mammoth** rubber band ball.

DID YOU KNOW?
The rubber used to make rubber bands comes from the sap of a rubber tree. Mayans and Aztecs of Central and South America were the first cultures to tap the rubber from several trees growing there. Explorers and colonists carried samples of these trees back to Europe.

Name_____ Date_____

■ Answer the questions.

1. What gave Waul the idea to make his rubber band ball? _____
_____

2. How did the people from the museum move the ball? _____
_____

3. **Mammoth** means:
   A. small
   B. huge
   C. rough
   D. rubbery

4. Circle *T* for true or *F* for false.

   A. Rubber band balls are made of rubber bands and glue.   T   F

   B. Rubber bands are made from the sap of a tree.   T   F

   C. Waul's rubber band ball is on display in his driveway.   T   F

5. Have you ever made something based on something you saw? Explain your answer.
_____
_____
_____

6. Do you think that Waul's rubber band ball would bounce? How could you test the giant ball to see if it would?
_____
_____

■ Choose one extension activity.

A. Waul had to start with one rubber band to begin making the giant ball. Start with one rubber band and make a rubber band ball of your own. How big will yours be?

B. Research other products that are made from the sap of a rubber tree.

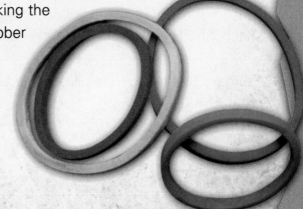

97

MILES-O-MOWING

■ Read the passage.

Longest Lawn Mower Ride, February 14, 2001

This road trip could be called a lawn trip. Gary Hatter (USA) drove across the country on his riding lawn mower. Hatter holds the Guinness World Records™ record for the Longest Lawn Mower Ride. He drove for 260 days and covered 14,594 miles (23,487.5 km).

Hatter started his lawn mower adventure on May 31, 2000. He began in Maine and kept on going. He drove through 48 states and parts of Canada and Mexico. He even went down Broadway in New York City. He said that people there **gazed** at him as if he were in a UFO. People stopped to stare and wanted to touch the lawn mower. He ended his trip in Florida on February 14, 2001.

Hatter did not take on the journey alone. He had the aid of his son. Gary Junior drove ahead of him carrying snacks, clothes, and gas in his car. They drove from three to ten hours each day. The mower could travel up to nine miles (14 km) per hour.

Hatter decided to take the trip because of back pain. He couldn't afford to pay for the back surgery that he needed. He decided to ride his mower across the country as a way to raise money for his surgery.

Name_____ Date_____

■ Answer the questions.

1. How fast can Hatter's lawn mower travel? _____

2. Where did Hatter go on his lawn mower? _____

_____

3. Which verb is <u>not</u> a synonym for **gazed**?

   A. gawked

   B. gaped

   C. laughed

   D. stared

4. Circle *F* for fact or *O* for opinion.

   A. Gary Hatter took the trip because of back pain.   **F**   **O**

   B. Gary Junior is a good son.   **F**   **O**

   C. Riding a lawn mower is a great way to travel.   **F**   **O**

5. Gary Junior drove his car ahead of Hatter carrying snacks, clothes, and gas. How else do you think that Gary Junior might have helped Hatter get through the trip?

_____

_____

6. Why do you think that people looked at Hatter as if he were driving a UFO through New York City? _____

_____

7. What are the main points of the passage?

_____

_____

_____

■ Choose one extension activity.

   A. Have you or someone you know tried to raise money for a cause? Write a list of other ways Hatter might have tried to raise money.

   B. How safe do you think it was for Hatter to drive across the country on his lawn mower? What safety issues do you think that Hatter had to consider and prepare for?

ROCKING THE AIR

■ Read the passage.
Most Air Guitar World Championship Wins, 2007

These guitar champions don't play a note. In fact, they don't even need actual guitars to perform. Zac "The Magnet" Monro (United Kingdom) and Ochi "Dainoji" Yosuke (Japan) hold the Guinness World Records™ record for Most Air Guitar World Championship Wins.

Air guitarists mime playing the guitar, which means that they pretend to play. They dance, make faces, sing, or lip-synch while they perform. Performers try to make it look like they are really playing. Usually air guitar is played to rock or heavy metal music.

The competition takes place in Finland. Performers from all over the world come to compete. The purpose of the competition is to **endorse** world peace. Contestants perform on stage in front of an audience and judges. Many performers say that they love feeling like rock stars.

Monro, an architect, won the competition in 2001 and 2002. Yosuke, a comedian, took the title in 2006 and 2007.

DID YOU KNOW?
The air guitar world championship in Finland started as a joke. It was meant to be a fun side attraction for the music video festival.

Name_____ Date_____

■ Answer the questions.

1. What equipment does a performer need to play the air guitar? _____
_____

2. What is the purpose of the Air Guitar World Championship competition in Finland?
_____

3. **Endorse** means:
   A. support
   B. enjoy
   C. appreciate
   D. discuss

4. Circle *T* for true or *F* for false.

   A. You need an electric guitar to learn to play the air guitar.   **T   F**

   B. Air guitarists try to make it look like they're really playing the guitar.   **T   F**

   C. The world championship takes place in the United Kingdom.   **T   F**

5. What do you think is the best way to learn to play an air guitar?
_____
_____
_____

6. What makes the guitar a good instrument to pretend to play? What other instruments might work?
_____
_____

■ Choose one extension activity.

A. Create an air guitar routine of your own. Can you make it look like you are really playing?

B. Describe ways in which the world championship competition may be making the world a more peaceful place.

BALANCING ACT

■ **Read the passage.**
Most Glasses Balanced on the Chin,
August 12, 2007

This Guinness World Records™ record-breaker would be a very popular waiter. Ashrita Furman (USA) balanced 81 one-pint glasses on his chin for 12.1 seconds. He performed his balancing act in his backyard in Jamaica, New York.

Furman is not new to Guinness World Record achievements. His first Guinness World Record was for doing 27,000 jumping jacks in 1979. Since then, he has set more than 250 Guinness records ranging from pogo stick jumping to yodeling. Furman even holds the record for breaking the most Guinness World Records! He currently holds around 100 records because many of his old records have been broken.

Ashrita, whose original name was Keith, says that he had no direction when he was younger. Then, he met a spiritual leader, Sri Chinmoy, became a follower, and changed his name. Furman says that he learned from Sri Chinmoy many valuable lessons that help him with his **feats**. Even if he is in pain while attempting to break a record, he uses focus to overcome it.

Furman manages a health food store in Queens, New York. He also coordinates travel for Sri Chinmoy's international peace conferences.

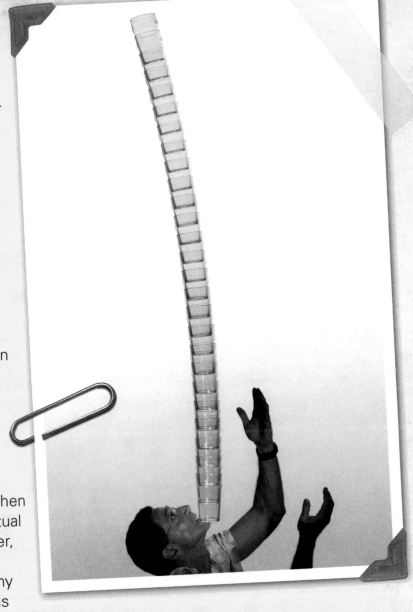

Name_____ Date_____

■ Answer the questions.

1. How many world records does Ashrita Furman currently hold? _____

_____

2. Where did Furman set the record for Most Glasses Balanced on the Chin?_____

_____

3. Which word is <u>not</u> a synonym for **feats**:
   A. accomplishments
   B. achievements
   C. failures
   D. successes

4. Circle *T* for true or *F* for false.

   A. Ashrita's name was Sri before he changed it.   T   F

   B. Sri Chinmoy works in a health food store.   T   F

   C. Ashrita Furman has set more than 250 world records.   T   F

5. Circle *F* for fact or *O* for opinion.

   A. Ashrita Furman has the record for breaking the most records.   F   O

   B. Ashrita couldn't break records if it weren't for Sri Chinmoy.   F   O

   C. Ashrita balanced 81 glasses on his chin.   F   O

6. How do you think that Furman is able to break so many records? Explain your answer.

_____

_____

■ Choose one extension activity.

A. Furman has set dozens of world records. Research some of the other records that Furman has broken.

B. Write a letter to Furman suggesting a new world record that you think he could set based on his numerous skills.

PORCUPINE FACE

■ Read the passage.
Most Clothespins Clipped on a Face, January 9, 2009

One look at Garry "Stretch" Turner (United Kingdom) showing off his Guinness World Records™ record is enough to make even the bravest person squirm. Turner set his record for the Most Clothespins Clipped on a Face. He beat his previous record by clipping on 160 clothespins.

Turner has skin that really stretches. He has a rare medical condition called Ehlers-Danlos syndrome. The condition makes his skin weak. Because of his condition, he has very loose and **elastic** skin.

Turner is able to pinch little bits of skin to get the clothespins on. He says that he is able to clip so many clothespins onto his face because of his elastic skin and his high tolerance for pain.

DID YOU KNOW?

David M. Smith invented the first clothespin in 1853. Clothespins were originally used to hang clothes on a line to dry. Over the years, they have been used for other things. People sometimes use them to keep their **nostrils** shut when something smells bad. And some people clip clothespins to their faces to beat records!

Name_____ Date_____

■ Answer the questions.

1. What is Garry Turner's nickname? _____
_____

2. How many clothespins did Turner clip on his face? _____
_____

3. Where are your **nostrils**? Name an animal with unusual nostrils. How are they unusual?
_____
_____

4. Another word for **elastic** is:
   - **A.** soft
   - **B.** tight
   - **C.** flexible
   - **D.** light

5. Circle *T* for true or *F* for false.

   A. Turner has a disease that a lot of people have.   T   F

   B. Clothespins were invented to clip onto people's noses when
   they smell something bad.   T   F

   C. Turner can handle pain easily.   T   F

6. What was the original purpose of clothespins? Have you ever used a clothespin in a different
way? What did you do with it?
_____
_____
_____

■ Choose one extension activity.

A. Clothespins have many uses. Design your own
unique use for a clothespin. Then, draw a picture
of your invention.

B. Turner can do many amazing things because of
his stretchy skin. Research Garry Turner to learn
what else he can do.

GOING BANANAS

■ Read the passage.

Largest Collection of Bananas, December 2, 1999

Ken Bannister (USA) is bananas for bananas. He is known as the Banana Man. Why? He holds the Guinness World Records™ record for the Largest Collection of Bananas. Bannister has 17,000 banana items. No, all of his banana stuff is not in his house. He owns the International Banana Club Museum. His collection is on display there.

Bannister began his **quest** in 1972. He handed out banana stickers for a fruit company. When he ran out of stickers, he made some of his own. The stickers were for the International Banana Club. Bannister handed out thousands of them.

Soon Bannister had an idea. He would offer degrees in Bananistry to people who sent him banana items. Eventually, Bannister had tons of items. He decided to start a museum. The museum opened in California in 1976.

Today, the Banana Club has members in 17 countries. Bannister says the purpose of the club is to make people smile. Anyone can join. The Banana Club is famous. It has been in magazines, in newspapers, and on television shows around the world.

Name_____ Date_____

■ **Answer the questions.**

1. When did Ken Bannister begin collecting banana items? _____
_____

2. How many countries are represented in the International Banana Club? _____
_____

3. Use a dictionary to find the definition of the word **quest** as it is used in this passage. What other words can you form with *quest* as the root word?
_____
_____

4. Circle *T* for true or *F* for false.

   A. Bannister is known as the Banana Kid.   **T**   **F**

   B. Anyone can join the Banana Club.   **T**   **F**

   C. The museum is in California.   **T**   **F**

5. Bannister handed out thousands of his own Banana Club stickers. Do you think this was a good way to get people interested in the Banana Club? What else could he have done to advertise the club?
_____
_____
_____

6. What is the purpose of the Banana Club? Do you think it is being achieved? How?
_____
_____
_____

■ **Choose one extension activity.**

   A. Bannister designed his own stickers for the International Banana Club. Design and draw a sticker for a club that you create.

   B. If you were going to start a museum, what would you collect? Write a list of items that would be on display in your museum.

© Carson-Dellosa

107

LIFE IN A BUBBLE

■ Read the passage.

Most People Inside a Soap Bubble, November 23, 2007

Have you ever blown a really big bubble? Sam Heath (United Kingdom) blows bubbles big enough to stand in! Sam, who goes by the name SamSam Bubbleman, holds the Guinness World Records™ record for Most People Inside a Soap Bubble. Fifty children stood inside Heath's gigantic bubble.

The amazing bubble was 11 feet (3 m) across and over 5 feet (1.5 m) high. First, the children stood on a platform above a pool of bubble **solution**. Heath dipped a 36-foot (11-m) metal hoop in the solution and raised it over their heads. The bubble **enveloped** the children for a few seconds before popping.

Heath performs in front of large audiences. He calls himself a "bubbleologist." He says that the secret of making bubbles is the mixture. Heath spent 20 years perfecting his own top secret solution and will not share his recipe. Heath also owns a bubble company. His company sells bubble solutions and equipment.

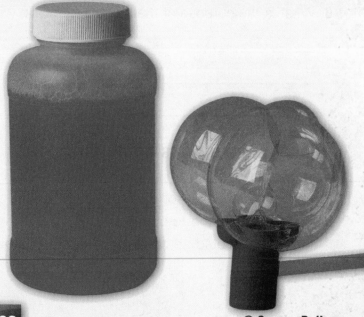

Name_____ Date_____

■ Answer the questions.

1. What does Sam Heath believe is the secret of bubble making?_____

_____

2. How tall was the giant bubble?_____

_____

3. A **solution** is a:

    A. mixture

    B. solid

    C. bubble

    D. mold

4. Use the verb **enveloped** in a sentence._____

_____

5. Circle *F* for fact or *O* for opinion.

    A. Bubbles are hard to make.   **F**   **O**

    B. Heath has the best bubble recipe in the world.   **F**   **O**

    C. Heath owns a bubble company.   **F**   **O**

6. Heath calls himself a "bubbleologist." What do you think that means?

_____

_____

7. Why won't Heath share his top secret recipe with anyone?

_____

_____

■ Choose one extension activity.

A. What do you think it felt like to be inside Heath's giant bubble? Write a poem describing how you might feel and what it would look like if you were inside the bubble.

B. What might Heath try to fit inside a bubble next? Draw a picture of something inside Heath's next giant bubble.

ONE GREAT GATOR

■ Read the passage.

Largest Toothpick Sculpture, March 22, 2005

If you have a small bit of food between your teeth, what do you do? You might try swirling your tongue around your mouth trying to force the **stubborn** morsel out. But, what if that doesn't work? Hopefully, you do not stick your finger in your mouth. Instead, you reach for a toothpick! Or maybe you reach for...an alligator named Alley?

Alley the alligator is made of more than three million toothpicks. Self-taught artist Michael Smith (USA) holds the Guinness World Records™ record for the world's Largest Toothpick Sculpture. He built Alley using toothpicks and wood glue. Smith spent three years building Alley. The toothpick gator is 14.76 feet (4.5 m) long and weighs 292 pounds (132 kg).

Though toothpicks aren't a typical sculpting **medium**, Smith loves working with them. Smith, also known as the Toothpick Man, even has a pair of toothpick eyeglass frames!

DID YOU KNOW?

Japanese toothpicks are pointed at only one end. The other end has a series of notches or grooves, which make it easy to snap off. The idea is that after using the toothpick you snap off the end to show that it has been used. Then, the tiny stub can be used as a little holder to keep the used toothpick off the table. Pretty neat!

Name_____ Date_____

■ Answer the questions.

1. What did Michael Smith use to build Alley? _____
_____

2. Which sentence does not use the word **stubborn** correctly?
   A. I could not get the stubborn stain out of my shirt.
   B. The stubborn mule would not budge.
   C. They were able to stubborn the weeds in the garden.

3. What do you think the word **medium** means as used in the third paragraph? Use the dictionary

   to check your answer. _____

   _____

4. Japanese toothpicks are different because:
   A. they are longer than American toothpicks.
   B. they are sharp on only one end.
   C. they are made of plastic.
   D. they are wider than American toothpicks.

5. Circle *T* for true or *F* for false.

   A. Michael Smith went to a special art school to learn how
      to sculpt with toothpicks.   T   F

   B. Toothpicks are only for picking food from between teeth. T   F

   C. Smith is also known as "Toothpick Timmy."   T   F

6. Why do you think toothpicks make a good building material?
   _____

   _____

■ Choose one extension activity.

A. Think of another simple household item and
   write a list of alternative uses for that item.
B. Toothpicks are not a typical artist's medium.
   Research other artists who have used odd
   items for their art.

LOTS OF DOUGH FOR A PIZZA

■ Read the passage.
Most Expensive Pizza

This record will make you hungry for more. Pizza is known as a quick and inexpensive meal. A large pizza pie normally costs around $15. But, this Guinness World Records™ record-breaking pizza does not come cheap. It is the most expensive pizza that you can buy, and it is available at a restaurant in London, England.

Each pizza costs about $178. The price depends on the availability of the most expensive topping, truffles. Truffles are an edible fungus, similar to mushrooms.

A famous chef, Gordon Ramsey, created this pizza. It is thin-crusted and wood fire–baked. Many fancy toppings **adorn** the pricey pizza. It is covered in a white truffle paste. It has onion puree, fontina cheese, baby mozzarella, pancetta, porcini mushrooms, and wild mizuna lettuce on top. The pizza is **garnished** with bits of a rare Italian white truffle. The truffle alone is worth $1,250 per pound (0.5 kg).

DID YOU KNOW?
Historians are not sure where the word *pizza* comes from. Some people think that it may have come from the German word *bizzo*, which means *mouthful*. Who would not want a mouthful of pizza?

112

Name_____ Date_____

■ Answer the questions.

1. What is the name of the chef who created the world's most expensive pizza?

_____

2. What toppings are on the record-breaking pizza? _____

_____

_____

3. Adorn means:

    A. beautify

    B. taste

    C. eat

    D. bake

4. Another word for **garnished** is:

    A. peeled

    B. covered

    C. decorated

    D. chopped

5. Circle *T* for true or *F* for false.

    A. Pizza is normally an expensive dish.   T   F

    B. Historians are not sure where the word *pizza* comes from.   T   F

    C. The most expensive pizza cost $1,250.   T   F

6. Do you think that the restaurant makes many of these pizzas? Why or why not?

_____

_____

■ Choose one extension activity.

A. Imagine that you are the head chef at a fancy restaurant. What could you put on your pizza to make it special? Name your pizza. Then, write a description for the menu.

B. Conduct a survey of your friends or family. Ask them to name their favorite pizza topping. Create a chart to display your results.

HAIRY EARS

■ Read the passage.
Longest Ear Hair, August 26, 2007

Some people love short hair, but others want as much hair as possible. Some want long eyelashes. Others would like long beards. Some even want long ear hair! If you think that ear hair can't grow very long, meet Anthony Victor (India). He holds the Guinness World Records™ record for Longest Ear Hair. In 2007, the longest hair in his ear measured an **impressive** 7.12 inches (18.1 cm).

Victor is proud of his ear hair. He has been working on it for a long time. When he was a teacher, his students noticed his ear hair. They called him "the ear-haired teacher."

Ear hair does not usually grow very long in children, but as people get older, the hair **follicles** in their ears tend to become more active. This is particularly true for men. No one knows for sure why this happens. Doctors suspect that it has something to do with the changes in body chemicals as people age.

Many men cut off their ear hair, or they ask a barber to trim it for them. Some people, however, value their long ear hair. At least two other men are hard at work growing their ear hair. Each one hopes to take over the title from Victor. By the time that you read this, one of these men might have ear hair measuring longer than Victor's. It may make you wonder: how much pride is there in having the second-longest ear hair in the world?

■ Answer the questions.

1. People tend to grow more ear hair as they _____ .

2. What nickname did Anthony Victor's students give him? _____
_____

3. What does the term **follicles** mean? What animals can you think of that have no hair follicles?
_____
_____

4. What is an antonym for the adjective **impressive**?
   A. stunning
   B. breathtaking
   C. spectacular
   D. ordinary

5. Why would it be surprising for a child to hold the Guinness World Record for longest ear hair?
_____
_____

6. Make a prediction about what Anthony Victor will say if someone breaks his Guinness
   World Record.
_____
_____

■ Choose one extension activity.
   A. Write a song about long ear hair.
   B. Draw three pictures of different ear
      hairstyles for Anthony Victor.

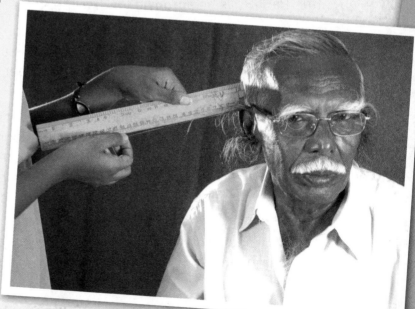

ROBO-SITTER

■ Read the passage.
Earliest Robot Babysitter

Will the babysitters of the future be robots? Japanese computer company NEC thinks so. They invented PaPeRo, which holds the Guinness World Records™ record for Earliest Robot Babysitter. PaPeRo is an **acronym** for "Partner-type Personal Robot."

PaPeRo is egg-shaped and 15 inches (38 cm) high. Children being babysat by the robot wear a transmitter and a wireless microphone. This allows the robot to track children's movements. PaPeRo can move 8 inches (20 cm) per second. The robot also can speak. It has 3,000 words in its vocabulary.

PaPeRo has cameras for eyes and microphones for ears. The microphones detect and recognize speech. The cameras help the robot recognize faces and surroundings. They also allow PaPeRo to take digital pictures. The pictures can be sent to a parent's phone or a computer. PaPeRo also has a phone. Parents can call PaPeRo, and it will find the children. Parents can also send text messages and talk to children through the speakers and microphones.

The company says that the robot can develop a personality depending on how it is treated. They even claim that if you speak to the robot nicely and stroke its head sensors, it will learn to love you!

Name_____ Date_____

■ Answer the questions.

1. What is PaPeRo?_____

_____

2. What does a child have to wear if being babysat by PaPeRo? _____

_____

3. Circle *F* for fact or *O* for opinion.

  A. PaPeRo is 15 inches (38 cm) high.   F   0

  B. PaPeRo has cameras for eyes.   F   0

  C. Children love PaPeRo.   F   0

4. What is an **acronym**? Create a new name for PaPeRo. What acronym would you use?

_____

_____

5. Do you think robots are the babysitters of the future? Compare and contrast a robot babysitter to a human one.

_____

_____

_____

6. What are the possible problems with having a robot watch a child? Would you want a robot to be your babysitter?

_____

_____

■ Choose one extension activity.

  A. Imagine that you are one of the creators of PaPeRo. Write a speech to convince a parent to use PaPeRo as a babysitter for a night.

  B. Research other robots that do the work of humans. What are they used for?

RATTLE-SNACK

■ Read the passage.

Most Rattlesnakes Held in the Mouth, December 20, 2008

Jackie Bibby (USA) definitely is not afraid of snakes. He has had a mouthful of them! Bibby earned the Guinness World Records™ record for holding the most rattlesnakes in his mouth. He held 11 rattlesnakes by their tails in his mouth for 10 seconds.

Bibby has gotten cozy with rattlers in more ways than one. He has shared a sleeping bag with 108 rattlesnakes and shared a bath with 75. Bibby has handled snakes since 1968. He loves them. He even is the president of The Heart of Texas Snake Handlers.

Bibby does not recommend trying to break rattlesnake records unless you are an experienced snake handler. He has been bitten four times in 32 years. He says that the bites are extremely painful, and medical treatment can be very expensive.

Bibby wants to continue breaking rattlesnake records. Most of his family and friends think that this is weird. However, Bibby's girlfriend probably understands. She is a **rookie** snake handler, and sometimes she performs stunts with him.

DID YOU KNOW?

Adult rattlesnakes do not eat every day. They usually can go about two weeks between meals. Younger rattlesnakes eat about once a week.

Name_____ Date_____

■ Answer the questions.

1. How many snakes did Jackie Bibby hold in his mouth? _____

_____

2. What other stunts has Bibby done with rattlesnakes?_____

_____

3. What is a **rookie**?

    A. a type of snake

    B. someone who is new to an activity or job

    C. someone who likes animals

    D. snake food

4. Circle *T* for true or *F* for false.

    A. Bibby has been bitten four times.   T   F

    B. Bibby is tired of working with rattlesnakes.   T   F

    C. Bibby's family thinks it is sensible for Bibby to perform rattlesnake stunts. T   F

5. Bibby is a snake handler and the president of The Heart of Texas Snake Handlers. What are some traits that would make someone a good snake handler?

_____

_____

_____

6. Do you think that Bibby will break his Guinness World Record? Do you think that he will continue handling snakes and performing stunts? Why or why not?

_____

_____

■ Choose one extension activity.

A. Research rattlesnakes. Where do they live? How dangerous is their venom?

B. What questions would you like to ask Bibby? Write a letter to him.

CRASH MAN

■ Read the passage.
Most Crash Tests, 2003

Rusty Haight (USA) is not afraid of bumps in the road. He holds the Guinness World Records™ record for Most Crash Tests. Haight has **endured** 846 collisions in cars.

Haight used to work as an investigator in San Diego, California. Now he works as a traffic-collision reconstructionist. In other words, he is a human crash-test dummy. Haight is like a car crash detective. He investigates accidents from the inside. He helps figure out why car crashes happen. He also works on ways to try to prevent them.

Before a crash test, accelerometers are hooked up to Haight and the car. Accelerometers are sensors that measure **acceleration**. Acceleration means how fast a car increases its speed. Once everything is in place Haight takes off and…crashes the car.

Haight is also a teacher. He teaches accident investigators and engineers about how crashes work. He also teaches high school students about traffic safety. Students seem to pay closer attention after he shows them videos of his crashes.

DID YOU KNOW?
The first crash test dummy was Sierra Sam. Sierra Engineering created Sierra Sam in 1949 for the U.S. Air Force. It was used to test helmets and oxygen masks.

120

Name_____ Date_____

■ **Answer the questions.**

1. What is Rusty Haight's official job title? _____

_____

2. What is the author's explanation of Haight's job? _____

_____

_____

3. What is another word for **endured**?
    A. celebrated
    B. crashed
    C. survived
    D. rode

4. What is **acceleration**? _____

5. Circle *T* for true or *F* for false.

    A. Haight is the principal at a high school.   T   F

    B. Haight crashes cars for a living.   T   F

    C. Haight once worked as an investigator in San Diego.   T   F

6. The author states that Haight investigates car accidents from the inside. What do you think that means? What are the benefits of this?

_____

_____

7. What is the primary purpose of Haight's work?_____

_____

■ **Choose one extension activity.**

A. How does Haight make sure that he stays safe through all those crashes? What do you think he does to protect himself?

B. Why do you think high school students pay closer attention to Haight after he shows them videos of his crashes? Do you think that this is a good way to teach students about safety? How would you react if you saw a video like that?

GUINNESS WORLD RECORDS

SCREAMING DIVA

■ Read the passage.

Loudest Scream, October 2000

Some people say that screaming is bad for your voice but good for your heart. They must have met Jill Drake (United Kingdom) firsthand. Jill Drake is a classroom assistant who has the world's Loudest Scream.

A **decibel** (dB) is the unit used to measure the volume of a sound. The sound of silence is 0 decibels. A conversation between two people is around 60 decibels. And, a jet engine measures 120 decibels.

Ms. Drake discovered her unique talent by accident. Her friends took her to a screaming competition. When she heard some of the other competitors, Jill decided to give it a try. Her scream measured a powerful 129 decibels. Jill's scream is louder than a jet engine!

How does a person become a "screamer"? Here are some tips:

- Warm up. Just like athletes warm up their muscles, you should warm up your voice.

- Scream from your **diaphragm**. Fill your lungs with air and let the diaphragm push up the scream

- Practice. Like anything, screaming takes practice.

- Finally, remember to scream outside. That is something your parents and any classroom teacher or assistant will appreciate.

Name_____ Date_____

■ Answer the questions.

1. For what is Jill Drake famous? _____

_____

2. What is a **decibel**? _____

_____

3. Circle *T* for true or *F* for false.

    A. Jill Drake went to the screaming competition to win.   **T**   **F**

    B. A jet engine is louder than Drake's scream.   **T**   **F**

    C. Drake is a classroom teacher assistant.   **T**   **F**

4. How would you compare and contrast Jill's scream to other loud sounds?

_____

_____

_____

5. The author offers tips on screaming. One tip is to use your **diaphragm**. Where is your diaphragm? Why is it an important tool in screaming?

_____

_____

_____

■ Choose one extension activity.

A. What is the loudest noise ever recorded? Create a graph displaying the different decibel levels for this and various other sounds.

B. Acoustics is the science that studies sound. Acoustics is an important part in the design of theaters, stadiums, and recording studios. Find out more information about acoustics. Design your own theater, stadium, or recording studio using what you learn.

Name_____ Date_____

REVIEW: WILD, WACKY & WEIRD

■ **Unscramble each word. Use the clues in parentheses to help you. Then, use the boxed letters to find the secret word that means "an increase of speed."**

1. tomhamm (huge)

2. tealsic (stretchy)

3. solefillc (hair roots)

4. dezag (stared)

5. bedilce (measures sound)

6. sequt (a long search)

7. kooire (new at a job)

8. rodan (to decorate)

9. fesat (amazing deeds)

10. lootsinu (liquid mixture)

11. notrubbs (difficult to move or remove)

12. myacorn (formed from initials)

Name_____ Date_____

REVIEW: WILD, WACKY & WEIRD

■ **Use the clues to complete the puzzle.**

ACROSS

2. A dentist's favorite alligator
4. Sam Heath calls himself this.
6. New Yorker: "Is that a mower or a _____?"
7. Years to make Waul's rubber band ball
9. Most Guinness World Records holder _____ Furman

DOWN

1. Babysitter of the future?
3. Garry Turner's nickname
4. Send something related to this for your degree in bananistry.
5. You don't need one to compete in Finland.
8. Original word for pizza?

ANSWER KEY

Page 11

1. about the size of Lana's thumb;
2. Toy Group; 3. A; 4. D; 5. T, F, F;
6. Answers will vary.

Page 13

1. a prehistoric mammal related to mammoths; 2. to get food and to fight; 3. A; 4. T, F, T; 5. to die off, Answers will vary but may include dodos and dinosaurs. 6. mammoth, elephant, Answers will vary but may include tusks, trunk, large size, both are mammals.

Page 15

1. Great Dane; 2. Answers will vary but may include large, sweet, gentle, friendly, loving. 3. Answers will vary but may include eats 110 pounds of food every week and sleeps in his own queen-size bed. 4. from the pads of the paws to the tops of the shoulders; 5. F, T, F; 6. A; 7. Answers will vary but may include that he has been on TV shows and in magazines, and he has his own Web site and social Internet pages.

Page 17

1. Answers will vary but may include official law enforcement work dog.
2. her owner, Sheriff Dan McClelland;
3. A; 4. O, F, F; 5. Benefits: Answers will vary but may include: she can fit in small places easily, Disadvantages: Answers will vary. 6. Answers will vary.

Page 19

1. Chianina ox; 2. Roman; 3. B; 4. T, T; 5. O, O, F; 6. Answers will vary.

Page 21

1. Africa, the Middle East, and western Asia; 2. its own weight in food or less than one ounce; 3. Answers will vary. 4. A; 5. F, T, F; 6. Answers will vary.

Page 23

1. Central and South America; 2. by whimpering, clicking, purring, and barking; 3. B; 4. F, T, F; 5. "master of grasses," Answers will vary but may include they eat mostly grass and aquatic plants. 6. Answers will vary.

Page 25

1. reserve deputy sheriff; 2. goes on patrol, attends events, participates in parades, promotes safety, and encourages people to stay off drugs; 3. D; 4. B; 5. O, F, F; 6. Answers will vary.

Page 27

1. Scientists estimate that he is between 70 and 80 years old. 2. They were hunted for meat and goats ate away at their habitat. 3. D; 4. F, F, T; 5. He is the only known living member of a subspecies of Galápagos giant tortoises. 6. Answers will vary.

Page 29

1. a large poisonous lizard; 2. enough to kill two people; 3. B; 4. poisonous, Answers will vary. 5. F, T, T; 6. Answers will vary.

Page 31

1. off the north coast of Iceland; 2. The Ming dynasty ruled China at the time Ming the Clam was born. 3. B; 4. F, T, T; 5. "tiny tape recorders"; 6. Answers will vary.

Page 33

1. by jumping the highest of any pig (27.5 inches, 70 cm); 2. smart, friendly, playful and they love attention;
3. animals that eat plants and meats, Answers will vary. 4. B; 5. T, T, F;
6. Answers will vary.

Page 35

1. a tan and white boxer; 2. C; 3. D;
4. first place in an ugly dog contest, second place in Stupid Pet Tricks, and second place in an owner-pet look-alike contest, Answers will vary.
5. Answers will vary. 6. the owner-pet look-alike contest, Answers will vary.

Page 36

Secret Message: Record-Breaking Animals; Record-Holders' Names: Lonesome George, Boo Boo, Giant George, Midge, Fiorino, Bert, Ming, Kotetsu, Brandy

Page 37

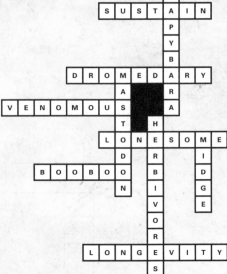

Page 39

1. Four; 2. 460 feet (140 m) high;
3. A; 4. T, F, T; 5. The doors had to be big enough for the rockets to fit through, No; 6. because of the building's enormous size

Page 41

1. 5 feet 2 inches (157 cm); 2. 6 feet tall (1.8 m); 3. C; 4. F, F, T; 5. she didn't fit on her father's motorbike, Answers will vary. 6. Answers will vary.

Page 43

1. 105,000 pink carnations; 2. a walkathon; 3. revealing the ribbon for the first time; 4. to remind people about a cause, Answers will vary.
5. Answers will vary.

Page 45

1. an operation that replaces the heart and lungs; 2. to bring oxygen into the blood and push carbon dioxide out; 3. B; 4. A; 5. T, F, F; 6. Answers will vary.

Page 47

1. a dramatic view of cliffs, waterfalls, and the Naruko-gawa Gorge;
2. Kokonoe, Japan; 3. A; 4. B;
5. dreams, Answers will vary.
6. Answers will vary.

Page 49

1. 20 kilohertz; 2. grasshoppers and crickets; 3. sounds that are higher than a person can hear; 4. T, F, T; 5. A; 6. an invertebrate animal with jointed limbs, a segmented body, and an exoskeleton made of chitin, Answers will vary.

Page 51

1. It looks like a ship coming through a wave. 2. 6.3 million gallons (24 million L); 3. C; 4. F, T, F; 5.–6. Answers will vary.

Page 53

1. 0.47 inch (12 mm); 2. the ability to pop out one's eyes; 3. A; 4. C; 5. F, F, F; 6. She was hit in the head with a hockey mask, Answers will vary.

Page 55

1. B; 2. F, T, F; 3. A; 4. endurance, Answers will vary. 5. a four-legged creature, Answers will vary. 6. Answers will vary but may include BigDog will not need to be fed, but it will need complex mechanical maintenance. 7. Answers will vary.

Page 57

1. He was inspired by a Chinese priest. 2. B; 3. 6 years; 4. D; 5.–7. Answers will vary.

Page 58

Secret word: pedestrian; 1. transplant; 2. recommend; 3. resident; 4. quadruped; 5. stature; 6. ultrasounds; 7. arthropod; 8. stamina; 9. amazed; 10. enormous

Page 59

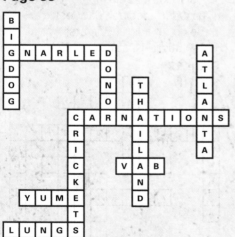

Page 61

1. an edible fungus; 2. Both are fungus, Answers will vary but may include mushrooms grow above ground, truffles grow beneath it in the roots of trees. 3. D; 4. O, F, O; 5. T, F, T; 6. Answers will vary.

Page 63

1. when there is a giant release of electricity, usually during a thunderstorm; 2. Florida; 3. C; 4. F, T, T; 5. in Shenandoah National Park, Answers will vary. 6. indoors, water and metal objects

Page 65

1. 14,000 Hawaiian plants; 2. Wahiawa, Oahu, Hawaii; 3. B; 4. T, F, F; 5.–6. Answers will vary.

Page 67

1. worked hard on the car, added special parts to give the car more power; 2. the terrain, huge rocks, sand, glaciers, and snow; 3. A; 4. B; 5. The higher a person goes, the thinner the air becomes, Answers will vary. 6. Ojos del Salado which means "eyes of the salty mountain", Answers will vary. 7. Eduardo Canales, Answers will vary.

Page 69

1. southeastern United States; 2. 140 mph (225 km/hr.), 74 mph (119 km/hr.); 3. A; 4. A; 5. T, T, F; 6. The storm quickly progressed from the lowest rating to the highest possible rating.

Page 71

1. Squash, celery, kale, lettuce, spinach; 2. No, their flavors are not as rich as smaller vegetables; 3. B; 4. O, O, F; 5.–6. Answers will vary.

Page 73

1. 224.7; 2. by how long it takes a planet to completely rotate; 3. A; 4. F, F, F; 5.–6. Answers will vary.

Page 74

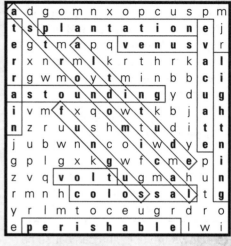

Page 75

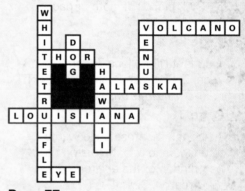

Page 77

1. an organization that helps cancer patients and their families; 2. his neighbor; 3. Answers will vary but may include a jump on a U-shaped ramp where the skater keeps the body facing the ramp or obstacle. 4. B; 5. T, F, F; 6. Answers will vary.

Page 79

1. 8 basketballs spun simultaneously; 2. 28; 3. A; 4. T, F, T; 5. The balls spin on top of nails in a special frame; 6. Answers will vary.

Page 81

1. youngest person to win the Wild West Arts' Texas Skip Race; 2. his mother; 3. D; 4. T, T, F; 5. Answers will vary.

Page 83

1. a team of four go-kart drivers (Russell Crowe, Joe Flay, Simon Rudd, and Tom Huxtable); 2. Answers will vary but may include small, open, four-wheel, motorized; 3. B; 4. F, T, F; 5. better for speed than distance, Answers will vary. 6. Answers will vary. 7. four, Answers will vary.

Page 85

1. He switched direction every 50 cartwheels. 2. more than 28; 3. D; 4. D; 5. O, O, F; 6. Answers will vary.

Page 87

1. a break-dance move where dancers rotate their bodies in the air while staying in contact with the ground; 2. slows the spin and can cause pain; 3. B; 4. T, F, T; 5. Answers will vary. 6. using pieces of cloth or pads for protection

Page 89

1. 33 feet (10 m) long 7 feet (2.15 m) wide; 2. Sherman Poppen; 3. A; 4. T, T, F; 5.–6. Answers will vary.

Page 91

1. about 2 months; 2. He wants to encourage people to stop the destruction of the environment in the Amazon. 3. A; 4. F, T, F; 5.–6. Answers will vary.

Page 93

1. Irwindale Speedway in California; 2. inside or next to the wheel; 3. A; 4. B; 5. O, F, F; 6. one, Answers will vary. 7. Answers will vary.

Page 94

1. aspire; 2. simultaneously; 3. aptitude; 4. prestigious; 5. landslide; 6. literal; 7. origin; 8. persuade; 9. continuous

Page 95

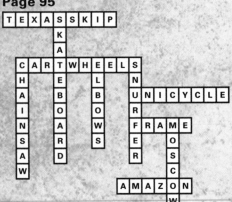

Page 97

1. Waul got the idea to make the ball after seeing on TV a giant rubber band ball dropped from an airplane. 2. with a crane and a flatbed truck; 3. B; 4. F, T, F; 5.–6. Answers will vary.

Page 99

1. 9 miles (14 km) per hour; 2. from Maine to Florida, through 48 states and parts of Mexico and Canada; 3. C; 4. F, O, O; 5.–6. Answers will vary. 7. Answers will vary but may include Gary Hatter rode to raise money for back surgery or he holds the record for Longest Lawn Mower Ride.

Page 101

1. none; 2. to endorse world peace; 3. A; 4. F, T, F; 5.–6. Answers will vary.

Page 103

1. around 100; 2. his backyard in Jamaica, New York; 3. C; 4. F, F, T; 5. F, O, F; 6. Answers will vary.

Page 105

1. Stretch; 2. 160; 3. at the base of your nose, Answers will vary. 4. C; 5. F, F, T; 6. to hang wet clothes on a line to dry, Answers will vary.

Page 107

1. 1972; 2. 17; 3. a search, Answers will vary. 4. F, T, T; 5. Answers will vary. 6. to make people smile, Answers will vary.

Page 109

1. the bubble mixture; 2. more than five feet (1.8 m); 3. A; 4. Answers will vary. 5. O, O, F; 6.–7. Answers will vary.

Page 111

1. three million toothpicks and wood glue; 2. C; 3. Answers will vary but may include a material used to create something. 4. B; 5. F, F, F; 6. Answers will vary.

Page 113

1. Gordon Ramsey; 2. White truffle paste, onion puree, fontina cheese, baby mozzarella, pancetta, porcini mushrooms, wild mizuna lettuce, and bits of a rare Italian white truffle; 3. A; 4. C; 5. F, T, F; 6. Answers will vary.

Page 115

1. get older; 2. ear-haired teacher; 3. a sheath of cells and connective tissue surrounding the root of a hair, Answers will vary. 4. D; 5. Ear hair does not usually grow long in children. 6. Answers will vary.

Page 117

1. the first robot babysitter; 2. a transmitter and a wireless microphone; 3. F, F, O; 4. a word formed from the initial letters of other words, Answers will vary. 5.–6. Answers will vary.

Page 119

1. 11; 2. shared a sleeping bag with 108 rattlesnakes, shared a bath with 75 rattlesnakes; 3. B; 4. T, F, F; 5.–6. Answers will vary.

Page 121

1. traffic-collision reconstructionist; 2. Answers will vary but may include: human crash-test dummy, car crash detective, investigates accidents from the inside, helps figure out why car crashes happen, works on ways to prevent them; 3. C; 4. how fast a car increases in speed; 5. F, T, T; 6. Answers will vary. 7. He helps figure out why crashes happen and how to prevent them.

Page 123

1. the loudest scream in the world; 2. the unit used to measure the volume of a sound; 3. F, F, T; 4. Answers will vary. 5. below the lungs, Answers will vary.

Page 124

Hidden word: acceleration; 1. mammoth; 2. elastic; 3. follicles; 4. gazed; 5. decibel; 6. quest; 7. rookie; 8. adorn; 9. feats; 10. solution; 11. stubborn; 12. acronym

Page 125

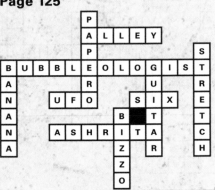